HERE
COMES
THE
SUN

Finding Your Way
Out of Depression

HERE
COMES
THE
SUN

Gayle Rosellini and Mark Worden

1817

A Harper/Hazelden Book

Harper & Row, Publishers, San Francisco

Cambridge, Hagerstown, New York, Philadelphia, Washington
London, Mexico City, São Paulo, Singapore, Sydney

FIRST HARPER & ROW EDITION PUBLISHED IN 1988.

Library of Congress Cataloging in Publication Data

Rossellini, Gayle.
    Here comes the sun.

    "A Harper/Hazelden book."
    Bibliography: p.
    1. Depression, Mental. I. Worden, Mark. II. Title.
RC537.R64   1988   616.85'27   88-45155
ISBN 0-06-255493-X

---

88 89 90 91 92 BANTA 10 9 8 7 6 5 4 3 2 1

FOʀ LUCILE CARTER WORDEN

A tough-minded optimist for over 80 years

CONTENTS

I'd rather learn from one bird how to sing
than teach ten thousand stars how not to dance

— e. e. cummings

PREFACE

This is not a book crammed with scientific facts and data about depression. We have taken the scientific facts and data into account, but current knowledge about the causes and cures of depression is in its infancy.

We have learned most from our own experiences with depression and from listening to the experiences of others. We believe one good example is worth ten pages of statistics, but we make no claim that the examples we have presented are typical, representative, or infallibly true of most depressed people.

The people we have used to illustrate aspects of depression are real people. We have not used their real names, and we have in all cases disguised other clues to their identities. In one or two instances we have drawn a composite portrait to illustrate some facet of depression.

We consider this book to be a philosophy of coping with depression, rather than a work of research, psychology, or medicine. As with any philosophy, we have gleaned ideas from a variety of other sources and combined them with our own thoughts. Our goal is to offer practical ideas to the troubled man or woman who is capable of happiness, but who does not know how to achieve it.

All we can claim for these ideas is that they are confirmed by our own experience and observation, and that they have increased our own peace of mind whenever we have acted in accordance with them. We hope they will do the same for you.

Chapter One

Hope Rekindled

Linda's Story

The two things Linda remembered later about that night were the unbearable feelings of guilty worthlessness festering deep inside her and the strange slow-motion precision of those final seconds before she crashed her car into the tree. But as time passed — weeks and months of healing — it was the absurdity of what she had done that kept coming back to her.

Why had she hated herself so much?

Why had she wanted to die?

At the time of her accident — no, let's call it by its right name — at the time of her suicide attempt, Linda's reasoning had a stark simplicity about it. *She was a failure.* An utter and complete failure in every dimension of her life — in marriage, in motherhood, and in her career.

Her husband didn't love her anymore. She knew it, she could feel it and see it in everything Danny did. And why should he love her? Why should he love a failure?

Her kids . . . they meant everything to her. But with the way things were, they'd probably be better off without her. They had their own lives now and they didn't show any respect for her at all. *If I died,* Linda brooded, *they'd get over it and that would be better for them than having to live with a mother like me.*

Oh, there was much more, much more. More bleak thoughts, more failures. They played in Linda's mind like a tape recording endlessly repeating, over and over. *You can't run the house right, you can't take care of the kids right, you can't do anything right.*

Making everything worse was Linda's certainty that her incompetence extended beyond family matters and into every aspect of her life, including her work. With agony she remembered the previous winter, a time of humiliation when she'd botched a big assignment at work. The manager had tried to make her feel better by saying everyone was entitled to a few mistakes. He'd smiled and tried to make light of it, but Linda knew she'd gone way down in his estimation. Just seeing him at work now was awful.

Linda's husband didn't know about her job problems. He'd be furious with her if he found out, if she lost her job, if she embarrassed the entire family by failing so miserably. She'd tried to make things right, again and again, but it seemed like once you got behind, it was impossible to ever catch up.

Maybe there were extenuating circumstances. Maybe there were good, acceptable reasons for her mistakes and blunders. Maybe not. The fact was that she had screwed up and that made her hate herself. She had prayed, had asked God for guidance, but it seemed like not even God was listening anymore.

As winter turned into spring and summer, Linda said nothing to anyone about her feelings and her fears. She was too ashamed. But she wasn't so sure her supervisor was keeping quiet. Linda thought she sensed a certain coolness from her co-workers. Did they stop talking when she came into the room? Did they look at her strangely? Were they checking up on her?

The stress of just getting through each day was becoming unbearable. *I'm so tired,* Linda kept thinking. It was a recurring punctuation to the rest of her thoughts.

She was spending a lot of time thinking about her childhood. Her upbringing had left her with a rigid and demanding conscience — perhaps too rigid, too demanding. Now, Linda's whole value system was crumbling under the burden of her failures. She couldn't think straight, couldn't rest.

She was losing weight and losing sleep, crying into her pillow at night, remembering New Jersey, and growing up, and the years her father drank too much and she knew he was destroying the family — knew it half apathetically because there wasn't anything she could ever do that made it different, and half in a wild soul-wrenching rage that she didn't dare show to another living being.

She recalled times as a teenager when she wanted to scream, fly across the room, to punish, to destroy, to stop all the pain in herself, in her parents, in the family. But she had never done it, never done anything. It wasn't her father who stopped her, or her mother, either. It was just an overpowering sense of futility about the way things were. Maybe it was the sense of futility, the helpless feeling, that made her first start hating herself.

As soon as she was old enough, she started making plans to get away, get out on her own where things would be different. And she had. She'd met Danny and they had fallen in love and gotten married and things had been better. How had she done that? How had she made the break? And why had things gone so terribly wrong?

What was she going to do? Why did these questions keep creeping into her mind, waking her up in the bleak predawn hours? She was so tired. She needed to sleep, but couldn't. Every night she lay in bed beside her husband. She couldn't understand how he could sleep so peacefully while the silent tears burned her face and soaked into the pillow.

Why didn't he wake up? Why didn't he pay attention? Why didn't he help her? Why didn't he make everything better? So many whys . . .

But if Danny stirred, Linda turned stiffly away. She lay there rigid, not daring to move lest he should discover her tears and ask the questions she couldn't answer.

But Danny knew something was wrong. He wasn't blind. He'd urged Linda to see a doctor, but she refused.

"I'm not sick," she insisted. Besides, what could a doctor do to help her? "Yes, Doctor, I'd like a pill that would make me a whiz at work and an all-around wonderful Betty Crocker mother at home." The harsh truth was that she felt unworthy, unfit as a wife and mother, totally alone in a private hell and that was how it was always going to be.

Fifteen years ago she'd believed in love and in Danny and in a bright dream of the future. And here she was now, crying alone in the night. In another fifteen years she'd be 50. Her brown eyes would be lost in puffy wrinkles and the skin on her cheeks and neck would droop and shake when she talked. She'd probably be in menopause and running to the doctor for hormones and no man would want her because she'd be so dried-out and old and useless.

Linda lay in bed next to her husband. He slept soundly at four in the morning, and she felt more alone than she'd been in her life. *What's the use?* she kept asking herself. *It'll never get better. Never.* Her whole life was a lie. What did she have to live for? She asked herself that question with an agonized intensity, and inside her a voice seemed to answer: "You're no damn good. You ought to remove yourself from your family. Give them a chance to start over without you."

Silently, Linda crawled out of bed. She went downstairs, sat down at the kitchen table, and composed a note to her husband, telling him she loved him and the children, but things would be better this way. She wept as she wrote it. Inside her, a voice kept telling her to hurry, hurry. Though she was terrified of dying, it seemed simpler, easier, and more worthy than living. Not even bothering to put a coat on over her nightgown, Linda took her purse and car keys and left the house.

She sat behind the wheel of her little Chevy and carefully drove away from her neighborhood. She didn't want to be stopped by a cop, she didn't want to be stopped from doing what she had to do. On the edge of town where the big trees grew, Linda picked up speed. She pressed her foot down hard on the gas pedal and aimed the little car at the wide trunk of the big oak tree growing right there next to the road. It was all so strange, like a dream. The car moved in slow motion, each foot of movement distinct and separate in the glare of the headlights. "God, forgive me!" Linda screamed as the tree loomed in front of her. She could see a hole in the trunk, a nest for squirrels. She didn't want to kill those poor, innocent squirrels. At the last second, she jerked the wheel sharply to the left. She felt herself flying through the air, an agonizing pain in her shoulder and side. Then blackness.

Pain.

Linda regained consciousness in a hospital bed. She tried to move, but couldn't. Her arm and shoulder were encased in plaster.

A woman in a green smock looked down at her, quite a young woman with long hair in a thick braid down her back. "You're in the hospital, dear," the nurse said. "You're going to be all right."

All right. Linda made a sick croaking sound. *All right.* She was such a miserable failure she couldn't even kill herself right. Steady throbbing pain moved through her shoulder and into her arm as a solid wave of despair swept over her and carried her down.

"I want to die!" Linda screamed. "Oh, God, I hate myself. I want to die!"

The nurse put her hand on Linda's forehead. "I know you do," she said calmly. "And we're not going to let you. We're going to help you want to live. We're going to teach you to love yourself again."

Love yourself again.

No, I don't deserve to live, a voice somewhere inside Linda

moaned. Just leave me alone and let me die.

The nurse, her face full of a deep understanding, gently stroked Linda's forehead and hair. "Everything is going to be all right. We're going to help you learn to love yourself again."

Love yourself. Linda could not shake those words. She turned her face to the wall and cried. But this time, her eyes burned with tears of hope.

Hiding Depression

Linda was so filled with despair and self-hate that she felt she could no longer tolerate living. Deep depression had dogged her for months. Indeed, she had suffered bouts of depression on and off ever since she was a teenager. And like so many other depressed people, Linda tried to hide it from those around her.

Why? Why do we try to hide, deny, and cover up our despair instead of reaching out for help? The reasons are actually pretty basic:

1. *We feel ashamed.* When we are in the depths of depression, our thoughts and emotions can be so unrelentingly negative, dark, and ugly that letting people know what's going on inside us would be too terrible. We don't want people to think we are weak or awful people.

2. *We feel guilty.* Along with depression come deep feelings of failure, of being bad. We condemn ourselves for messing up our lives and we think everyone else blames us too.

3. *We're afraid we'll be punished.* Sometimes the people closest to us — our mates, children, co-workers, parents, and friends — react harshly if we show we have problems. They get angry, lecture us, and tell us to straighten up. Stern pep talks let us know our personal problems are unacceptable. Instead of an offer of help and understanding, we're afraid we'll get disapproval

and condemnation from the people we care about, so we hide our real feelings.

4. *We're afraid we'll be rejected.* Rejection is one of the punishments we fear most. We worry that if we express our feelings to the people we care about, they'd be so disgusted they'd stop loving us. Or if they did still love us, they certainly would not respect or like us very much. So, we live in constant fear of being abandoned by the people we love.

5. *We're afraid people will think we're crazy.* A depressed person's mind is disordered. When we're depressed, we view the whole world through a black filter. We tend to see only the negative, the bad, the ugly. But this doesn't mean we're crazy. We're confused, but most depressed people are still in contact with reality. We know our names and where we are, and approximately what time zone we're in. Yet, because we're so anxious and despairing inside, we worry that people will think we've gone completely off our rocker if we let them know what's going on in our minds and hearts.

6. *We feel alone and hopeless.* If there is any one thing that keeps us stuck in the bottom of our pit of despair, it's our feelings of total isolation and hopelessness. We come to believe that no one — not our mate or our parents or our friends, not a counselor or a minister or a doctor — no one can possibly understand or help us. We believe we are worthless and everyone knows it, and it's always going to be that way.

This belief is wrong.

Linda believed her situation was so hopeless that death was the only way out.

She was wrong.

The kindness of a hospital nurse rekindled Linda's lost sense of hope. Hope was the key that unlocked the prison of self-hate she had built around herself.

Today, Linda is physically and emotionally recovered. Her

fear, shame, and guilt are gone. She no longer lives in despair; instead, she has a positive outlook on life. She and her husband feel closer than ever and are taking great pride in seeing their children participate in school activities and sports. This transformation did not take place by magic. Linda had to work hard, she had to accept help, and she had to leave hopelessness behind.

Getting Out of Depression

If you are suffering from depression, or if you care about someone who is lost in despair, are you willing to break free from the bonds of hopelessness? When we feel hopeless, we are not right within ourselves, and as a result we lose touch with the help and love and joy available to us. But there is no need for us to continue in this unhappy and lonely state of mind.

The way out of depression is, first, to want out.

We cannot sit back and apathetically wait for our unhappiness to disappear like magic. We must actively work to understand and change the conditions, attitudes, and circumstances which contribute to our misery.

Second, we need to get help from a counselor, doctor, therapist, or even a wise and loving friend.

A good physical examination from a medical doctor who understands depression might be in order right in the very beginning of your recovery. Depression may arise from a physical disorder, and it's important to rule out physical sickness and disease at the outset. If you are depressed, you may be suffering from a biochemical imbalance in your brain. Simply put, this means depressed people frequently have a mixed-up brain chemistry, just like people with diabetes have a mixed-up blood sugar chemistry. And, just as a diabetic can be helped by insulin, a depressive can frequently be helped by a whole new array of antidepressant medications that are neither addictive nor intoxicating. We'll talk a lot more about this later.

We need to do some old-fashioned thinking, analyzing, and soul-searching.

"Good God!" the depressed person says dolefully. "I've been doing nothing but thinking and analyzing and soul-searching. I don't want to think anymore, I want relief!"

It's true, such a suggestion may sound strange to you because you've probably been in a constant state of morbid self-analysis for quite a long time now. Uncontrollable thoughts about your life and failures and betrayals may race through your mind all night long. In fact, one of the recognized symptoms of depression is preoccupation with all the bad things that have happened in the past and will probably happen in the future. So, you may be saying that you want to be able to stop thinking so much, not start thinking more.

But, you see, depressed people don't really think about or analyze their lives in rational or realistic ways. Instead, when we're depressed, we brood, sulk, worry, and fret. We dwell on the past, reliving the hurtful, shameful, or humiliating things that have happened to us, and we imagine a future filled with more of the same. We can actually end up making ourselves physically ill with our constant ruminations and our unrelenting negative brooding.

So, an important aspect of recovering from depression is learning how to think about our lives in a more positive way. If all we put into our minds is resentments, bitterness, hate, gripes, despair, and grudges, that's exactly what we will get out again. If we are miserable and depressed, or if we keep messing everything up, the chances are that we have become world-class experts in negative thinking.

One of our most important tasks will be learning how to turn our minds away from pain and suffering and toward happiness, peace, and the simple pleasures of everyday living.

We must create a powerful vision of ourselves in the present and the future — a whole new sense of where we are going, how we are going to get there, and the kind of person we would like to become.

This idea works in a simple way: by envisioning the life we want, we can more easily achieve our goal. But remember, visualizing a better life is more than dreaming or fantasizing, which often get us nowhere. Vision is the link between dream and accomplishment. Envisioning ourselves the way we would like to be — healthy, content, loved, and competent — is an important step toward a better life. An even more important step is taking ACTION.

We must bring our behavior into alignment with our vision.

If we want to be healthy and happy people, we must start *behaving* like healthy, happy people. We have to start taking care of ourselves — physically, mentally, emotionally, and spiritually.

Our message is this: *Depression can be overcome.*

Are you ready to start taking action toward a happier life now? We really can find happiness in this lifetime, but we'll have to travel over some bumpy roads to get from here to there. So far, everyone we know who has come back from depression says the difficulty in passage was worth the effort. Are you ready to start on that journey now?

Chapter Two

Signs and Symptoms

What is this thing called depression?

The way the word is bandied about in everyday conversation, you'd think we all knew exactly what was meant when a person says, "I'm so depressed." But do we?

Ellen: "I'm so depressed. I spilled coffee on my white dress and now I have to wear that old blue one to the party tonight. I feel just awful."

Leslie: "God, I'm so depressed. My mother died yesterday. This is the most awful thing that ever happened."

Alan: "I must have gotten up on the wrong side of the bed this morning. I'm really feeling down. It's gonna be one of those days."

Carl (after a long silence and a heavy sigh): "I am so damned depressed. My life is totally screwed up and it's not ever going to get better. Everything is awful."

Are these four people talking about the same thing? Or does Ellen really mean she is frustrated and irritated? She may indeed feel bad, but the bad feelings might go away if she gets a compliment on her appearance, or if she gets invited to dinner.

Leslie, on the other hand, feels bad for totally different reasons. She is suffering from completely normal and understandable sadness. Compliments won't change the way she feels about the sudden loss of her mother. After the initial

13

shock wears off, the healing powers of time can help bring Leslie out of her natural state of grief.

Alan truly feels low and blue. He gets these bad moods a couple times a month, but his blues are temporary and situational. He usually perks up after a day or so. Like Ellen, his spirits can be lifted by a pleasant change in routine — a call from a friend, or a good meal, or a romantic interlude.

Perhaps Carl is the only one of the four who is actually mired down in the long-term hopelessness and despair that signals depression. His bad feelings are impervious to situational changes; good news cheers him little. Carl's gloominess is impenetrable, an all-pervading melancholy that affects his whole life — his posture (slumping, listless), his facial features (down in the mouth), his behavior (lethargic, lifeless), his thinking (negativity, black thoughts, foreboding, doom), and his spirit. (Life's meaningless. Life's a bitch, and then ya' die.)

So, what's the difference between being sad or unhappy and being depressed? Distressing emotions such as sadness, anger, and fear are a part of natural life. Bad feelings come and go in all of us, along with the more positive feelings like joy, excitement, and happiness. All these emotions — the good and the bad — are desirable because they enhance our human potential, adding depth and meaning to our lives. When these emotions are based on a realistic perception of events around us, they flow freely, are experienced, then fade away to be replaced by other emotions that are appropriate to the inevitable changes that occur in every person's life.

Consider, for example, a friend of mine* named Paula. She was devastated when her husband, whom she loved very much, left her for a younger woman. Paula was grief-stricken, enraged, frightened, humiliated. After her husband moved out of their home, she sincerely believed she would

---

*We are writing of our clinical experiences. "I" or "My" can refer to either of the authors.

never be happy again. Self-pity overwhelmed her. "I don't know what I'm going to do. I just don't understand how he could do this to me," she said with a kind of despairing bitterness.

As the divorce proceeded and the property was split up, Paula found herself dissolving into crying jags at the slightest provocation. But after several months, her moods began to pick up again. Although she was living in greatly reduced circumstances, she started feeling hopeful about the future. She enrolled in the local community college to brush up her skills, and when she met men on campus, she found herself speculating about romantic possibilities.

To her great surprise, Paula discovered she was no longer feeling sad and miserable every day. She was beginning to enjoy life again.

Paula had experienced a perfectly normal and healthy period of sadness, grief, and anger over the end of her marriage. And she had come out the other end a stronger, more resilient, and deeper person. In many ways a different person altogether.

The point is this: *When something unpleasant happens to us, it's normal to feel distressing emotions for a while.*

Sadness that is a realistic response to loss or failure or pain involves a normal flow of feelings and therefore is limited in duration.

In depression, our distressing emotions take over. It's no longer a question of sadness or anger or fear coming and going; these unpleasant feelings become our very being. Our sadness persists or recurs indefinitely and our self-esteem plummets.

Take Irene, for instance. When I first met Irene in the summer of 1985, I was immediately struck by the air of great sadness around her. She had the look of a woman exhausted by suffering. She was about 50; and although her face was nearly unlined, her stooped posture and slow gait made her seem old.

As our conversation progressed, I learned that, like Paula, Irene had been deserted by a two-timing husband. She spoke of her pain, her anger, and how difficult it was to endure the pitying looks of the people who knew that her husband had deserted her for another woman.

My heart certainly went out to this unfortunate middle-aged divorcée. I asked Irene, "When did your husband leave?"

Irene looked at me forlornly and gazed off into the distance. "It was in the spring, which used to be my favorite season, but not anymore." She sighed deeply. "I'll never forget it. It was May 12, 1967."

Twenty years ago, and yet for Irene the betrayal took place yesterday. I realized Irene's problem was far different from Paula's. Paula had suffered normal sadness. Irene's morbid preoccupation with the past showed she was seriously depressed.

While everyone will be bruised a little by life, only some of us end up like Irene, crushed under the weight of despair and depression. We can't take it. Disappointments wound us terribly, criticism cuts us to the bone, everyday obstacles overwhelm us, and the future appalls us. We are more than sad; we are the depressed ones. And there are a lot of us.

Sadness is a normal emotion.

Depression is a distortion of a normal emotion.

Depression is sadness and anger blown out of proportion. Depression lives on feelings of resentment and injustice, it feeds on the pain of the past, and it sees no hope or relief in the future. *Depression is truly a disorder of the whole person, affecting our bodies, our thinking, our emotions, and our spirits.*

Now, here's something that may seem very odd, but is nonetheless true: A person can be severely depressed and not know it. How can this be? Well, it's simple — we fool ourselves. Let's look at some of the common excuse strategies we use to hide the truth from ourselves and others.

1. *We may insist our bad moods are entirely caused by our lousy job, or our unloving mate, or our desperate financial situation.* In other words, we blame outside factors for our unhappiness, refusing to consider the idea that it may be the other way around, that our depression contributes to problems on the job or in our relationships.

Barney had been severely depressed for about six months when his wife, Kate, dragged him into my office for marriage counseling. Barney radiated doom and gloom from every pore. Kate was baffled. Their marriage, she said, had been a good one for over ten years, then Barney suddenly seemed to change. He became moody and depressed. He wouldn't eat the meals she prepared, and he lost 30 pounds, dropping from a healthy 155 to a painfully thin 125. Unable to sleep at night, he prowled the house until dawn, then dropped into a deep slumber that made him regularly late for work. Kate and Barney hadn't made love in months. She complained that Barney seemed to be slipping away from her and withdrawing into a world of his own.

Barney had a one word response to Kate's complaints: "Crap." There was nothing wrong with him, he insisted, except that he lived with a woman who made his life a living hell with her criticism and nagging. And the new boss at work was a real turkey. "Hey," Barney told me, "you'd be a little moody, too, with all the crap I have to put up with."

But as Barney kept talking, it became apparent his problems at work and the difficulties in his marriage stemmed in large part from his depression, and were not the cause of it. Yet, he felt compelled to shift the blame away from himself and on to someone else — in this case, his wife and co-workers.

Barney's behavior is not unusual. Like many people, he believed emotional problems were a sign of a weak character, something to be ashamed of and denied. Although he knew something was terribly wrong with him, it was easier for him to hide his depression from himself than it was to admit to having an emotional problem, or, God forbid, a "mental disorder."

2. *We may blame our low feelings on physical illness.* This offers an easy explanation because depression has many physical effects. We may blame our low level of functioning on a virus we just can't shake, backaches, headaches, fatigue, joint pain, stomachaches, or general weakness.

I once worked regularly with a woman named Kenda who was one of the most unrelentingly negative people I've ever met. Over the years, at least seven different doctors had suggested that her many physical complaints were caused or exacerbated by chronic depressive illness. She ignored every one of them and went in search of yet another doctor who would fix her aches and pains and ills.

"I have cancer, I just know it," Kenda blurted out to me one day. She ripped open her blouse. "Feel this lump," she insisted. "Does it feel like cancer to you?" Over the next five months, three different doctors — a general practitioner, a gynecologist, and an internist — examined Kenda and assured her that not only did she not have cancer, there wasn't the slightest trace of a lump where she said she felt one growing.

As time passed, Kenda lost all of her physical vitality. Her thinking and conversation focused almost entirely on her bodily functions. She fretted about her bowels and commented frequently on her constipation and dry mouth. She suffered from pains in her joints, muscles, and back, and the discomfort kept her chairbound all the time. "It hurts too much to move," she complained.

Convinced she was being slowly eaten alive by some terrible disease, Kenda underwent test after expensive test, all of them negative. Finally, her pain had settled in her back. When a test showed no damage to the spine, she called her doctors "quacks and idiots." And she was even more distressed when a test for arthritis came up negative. Although medical treatment never brought her the slightest relief, she continued her search for any new doctor, test, or treatment that promised to make her feel better.

3. *We may believe it is our fate in life to suffer.* Religious or moral training that promotes the idea that people are basically evil can lead us to believe our emotional or physical pain is righteous punishment for our sinful nature.

Debbie was raised by parents who belonged to an obscure religious sect that preached the sinfulness of human pleasure. Whenever Debbie showed joy or delight, her parents punished her. When she was ten years old, she had a bicycle she loved to ride. She came home from school one day and found it chopped to pieces in the front yard. Her father had heard her laughing as she rode it down the sidewalk, so it had to be destroyed.

When she was twelve, Debbie brought home a stray puppy. She fell in love with the little dog, but showing affection for the stray puppy had been a fatal mistake. Her father made Debbie watch as he drowned the dog in a bucket.

Debbie developed a deep depression that followed her into adulthood. Her thinking and emotions were retarded. She felt heavy, slow, and tired all the time. Pressure seemed to build up in her head. Food, sex, and socializing interested her very little. Her existence was absolutely joyless. Debbie saw nothing peculiar with these symptoms and she was offended when her employer suggested she seek treatment. "We were born to suffer," she stated righteously. "I'll find happiness in another life."

Depression, then, can take many forms. But if we know what to look for, we can learn to recognize it. We can learn strategies to prevent depression, and we can learn how to deal with the depressions of friends and loved ones.

Many of the symptoms of depression are things you might not ordinarily associate with a depressive state. What follows are lists of some of the major symptoms a depressed person might experience. (While it's unusual for all these symptoms to be present in one person, a number of these symptoms added together form the disorder we call depression.)

Physical Complaints

- *Fatigue.* You may feel overly tired and lack your normal drive to get things done. Even routine tasks seem overwhelming and not worth the effort.
- *Changes in appetite.* You may lose interest in food and end up losing weight because eating is an unpleasant chore. Or you may feel constantly hungry, especially for junk food.
- *Sleep problems.* You may want to stay in bed a lot, though you have difficulty sleeping. You may wake up in the early morning darkness, feeling frightened, anxious, tearful, and worried. Poet Gregory Corso put it this way in "Zizi's Lament":

    O bitter damned night! you again! must I yet
    pluck out my unreal teeth
    undress my unlaughable self
    put to sleep this melancholy head?

- *Aches and pains.* You may find yourself suffering from chronic pain in the back, the head, or joints. The pain generally does not respond to medical treatment, and when one problem clears up, another usually takes its place.
- *Digestive problems.* A dry mouth, nausea, dry retching, and constipation are not unusual.
- *Loss of sex drive.* Interest in sex may drop to a low level. Impotence and the inability to achieve orgasm are common, as are menstrual irregularities.
- *General complaints.* Weakness, dizzy spells, chest pains, stomach cramps, difficulty in breathing, sweating, tingling in the hands and feet, headaches, and an odd pressure in the neck and head are all common physical reactions to depression.

Distortions of Thinking

- *Poor concentration.* Your mind wanders when you try to grasp new information. After reading a newspaper or talking to someone, you may find you have retained little or nothing. You can't keep your mind on what you're doing.
- *Poor memory.* You can remember things that happened ten or twenty years ago, but recent events are blurry. You might have trouble remembering directions or new phone numbers or appointments and promises.
- *Trouble in making decisions.* It's not only major decisions that give you trouble, but even minor choices seem overwhelming. What to fix for dinner or how many gallons of gas to buy can stump you.
- *Mental dullness.* Your thinking may seem slow and cumbersome. New and creative ideas evade you, and your thoughts seem to go in circles.
- *Dwelling on the past.* You may find yourself unable to stop ruminating about past events and how they might have turned out differently. This is especially troublesome at night and can keep you from sleeping.
- *Financial worries.* Unrealistic concerns about using up all your resources may plague you. You may go to extremes in your spending habits, either becoming miserly or extravagant. Even if you have a good income, you may worry about ending up a skid row bum or a bag lady.
- *Negative thoughts and urges.* You may find yourself constantly expecting disaster to strike. Fears that loved ones will be harmed or killed are frequent and you may sometimes have urges to strike out against the people around you.

Emotional Symptoms

- *Irritability.* All sorts of trivial things can set off your temper, making you impatient and snappish. You may also find yourself holding grudges long after the provocation is gone.

Here *Comes the Sun*

- *Overreaction.* A flood of uncontrollable emotions — fear, anger, embarrassment, sentimentality, and even laughter — can be triggered by small events. Your emotional responses are all out of proportion to the stimulus.
- *Tearfulness.* You may frequently find yourself on the verge of tears for what seems like no reason at all.
- *Guilt.* You may feel you're not living up to the proper standards of conduct and this belief fills you with guilt. You blame yourself not only for your own problems, but you have a tendency to feel responsible for the behavior and unhappiness of your family and friends.
- *Remorse.* You spend a lot of time thinking. "If only. . . ." You deeply regret things you should have done and didn't and the things you shouldn't have done, but did.
- *Loss of fond feelings.* You may discover affectionate feelings toward family and friends disappearing. You may be shocked to find you really don't care anymore. You may also feel those around you have rejected and betrayed your love.
- *Social isolation.* You withdraw into yourself. You have little desire to be with people. You avoid good friends. Though you may feel intensely lonely, it is much easier for you to be alone than it is to socialize.

Spiritual Emptiness
- *Lack of pleasure and joy.* The inability to experience enjoyment and pleasure in everyday life is the cornerstone of depression. While no depressed person suffers from all of the symptoms we have described, every depressive suffers from a profound lack of pleasure and enjoyment of life.
- *Indifference.* People, ideas, and events that once interested you may now seem boring. You may become self-absorbed and single-minded, showing little interest in anyone or anything that does not directly and immediately affect you.
- *Hopelessness.* You are convinced your situation will not improve and will probably get worse. The present is

22

unbearable and you think the future holds more of the same.

- *Existential malaise.* You may feel your existence is totally futile and without meaning. Life seems absurd or pointless, "full of sound and fury, signifying nothing."

- *Estrangement from God.* You may find yourself blaming God for your pain, arguing with Him or making deals. In your suffering, you may believe God has deserted you or He is punishing you for your sins and crimes.

- *Preoccupation with death.* You may begin to think (or hope) a terrible disease is destroying your body or your mind. You may become angry and suspicious with your doctors, believing they are incompetent or they're hiding the truth from you. You may taunt death by placing yourself in dangerous situations, going right to the edge of oblivion, then pulling back. Death both fascinates and terrifies you, and it is frequently on your mind.

- *Suicidal thoughts.* You may either think about specific ways of killing yourself or hope you won't wake up in the morning. In the deep stages of depression, death may seem like the only way out of an intolerable situation.

It is important to remember that no one person will suffer from all of these symptoms. However, *a lack of joy and pleasure in life is the cornerstone of depression.* This is the one symptom shared by all depressed people.

With all of the modern advances in medicine and psychology, one would think the diagnosis and treatment of depressive illness would be an easy task. It isn't.

Depression is a baffling and a cunning disorder. It can manifest itself in many different ways. Unfortunately for those of us who have felt its weight upon our shoulders, depression is not a clear-cut and simple little problem to diagnose or conquer.

But conquer it, we can.

With the treatments available to us today, over 80 percent of people who suffer from even chronic and severe depression can recover and lead healthy lives. An even higher percentage of those with milder depressions recover, usually in a relatively short time. We *can* find inner peace, contentment, and meaning in our lives.

Now, listen: I'm not promising nirvana. When we recover from depression we will still have hassles almost every day. We will feel sad at times, and we'll experience periods of grief and unhappiness. This is normal. *Problems are a natural part of life.*

So, yes, once we conquer depression, we will still have problems. But they will no longer overwhelm us. We will have what it takes to take it. When life dishes out a disaster (and it most assuredly will) we don't have to lapse into the downward spiral of severe and disabling despair. We can face life head on, and we can prevail. We can even be happy.

Let's take some time now to look at the major causes of depression and then let's get down to our real work — pulling ourselves up from the darkness and into the healing light of recovery.

Chapter Three

Why Me?

When depression recurs over and over again, or when it lingers on without let-up for weeks, months, and years, depressed people inevitably ask: *"Why me?* Why am I the one who has to suffer? I look around and I see other people smiling and laughing, I see others enjoying life, achieving what they want, and having a good time. Why can't I be like that?"

Well, you can. Even the most negative, depressed, unlucky, and miserable people can learn to enjoy life. They can become more positive and optimistic, they can change their luck and ameliorate their misery.

Of course, a depressed person will find this hard to believe. A person who has been depressed for days, weeks, and even months feels as if a gloomy pall has descended on life. Talk about zest and cheerfulness and enthusiasm sounds like gibberish to the depressed person. It sounds like a hollow, contrived kind of psychobabble. "They're just saying those things to try to cheer me up," the depressed person thinks, and bolsters his or her depression by brooding darkly on the insincerity of friends.

In conversations with clients and friends who have fallen victim to depression, some of the most frequently asked questions are, "Why am I this way?" or "Why do all these bad things happen to me?" or "Why am I so oversensitized to emotional pain?"

I'm always reluctant to address the issue of "Why" because when we ask "Why" questions we usually want simple answers. But simple answers always leave something out, and our explanations always include guesswork and supposition.

Most of the time we just don't know exactly why one person will be scarred by a particular experience and another will be strengthened. As the saying goes, "The same fire that melts the butter, boils the egg."

There are many views about why people become depressed. Some scientists and psychiatrists believe that depressive illness is caused by a chemical imbalance in the brain. Others insist unresolved emotional conflicts are to blame. Still others pinpoint stress, childhood trauma, or our competitive society.

And to muddy up the waters even more, we have to realize that not all depressions are alike. For example:

When Helen has a depressive episode she feels slow, tired, and mentally dull. Her emotional responses are delayed and flat. When people talk to her, it feels like the words have to travel a great distance to reach her. She stays in bed sixteen hours a day and feels hungry all the time. During one bout of depression, she gained 50 pounds in less than three months. Helen doesn't know why she gets depressed; the bad feelings seem to come from nowhere.

Roxie's depressions are nothing like Helen's. Her dark moods can usually be traced to something bad happening to her, like a disappointment, failure, or embarrassment. When this happens, she starts feeling nervous and jumpy, as if she can't sit still. Her mind races with terrible thoughts of bitterness, self-recrimination, and revenge. She can't sleep and the sight of food makes her want to throw up. If she tries to eat, it feels like her throat closes off. All she can seem to do is chain-smoke and drink wine. She feels guilty and worthless and broods about dying. Events that might shake another person up for a few hours or a few days can depress Roxie for months.

Marvin swings from euphoria to despair. In his high moods he feels expansive, powerful, and strong. His mind races with schemes and plans, and he's so excited he doesn't want to be bothered with sleep. Then clunk. Everything turns to ashes and dust, the world is black and life is futile. Sometimes, between his highs and lows, he'll feel good, like his life is on an even keel, then it'll be clunk again. Marvin drinks a lot when he's feeling down, but when he's flying high he doesn't want anything to interfere with the feeling.

Michelle feels neither up nor down. She just feels flat, like she's going through the motions of living. She doesn't feel all that terrible, but she can't remember feeling good for at least the last three years. Her back aches a lot and she's bored with her job, her boyfriend, and her apartment. She wishes something exciting would happen, but it never does. Life just goes on from day to day, as empty and boring as ever.

As you can see, depression affects different people in different ways. One person might lose weight, another might balloon up. Maybe you can't sleep, or you might want to sleep too much. You might suffer from black despair or wild elation, or you might simply suffer from a terrible emotional flatness.

To complicate the situation even more, there are dozens of medical labels and whole books of confusing terminology, all devoted to describing and explaining this thing we call depression.

A person could get really down just trying to figure out what to label their dark moods. When you get depressed should you call yourself "anhedonic"? Or would it be more accurate to say, "I'm dysphoric"? We may wonder, "Do I have an affective disorder or mood incongruency? Am I cyclothymic or dysthymic? Am I obsessive-compulsive or manic-depressive or hypochondriacal? Or does it really matter what label I use?"

I think most of us would be wise to leave the labels and the medical terms to the doctors and clinicians as they write up their case notes.

Right now, maybe all that's important is for you to know that you feel depressed. You have lost your zest for life. You no longer feel joy or pleasure in living, and you have been feeling unusually gloomy and low for more than a few weeks. Acknowledging to ourselves that something is seriously wrong with the way we are reacting to the daily demands of living is the first important step toward taking responsibility for our own future happiness.

Taking Responsibility for Your Life

In the beginning we said that the way out of depression is, first, to want out. *And to want out, we must first recognize that something is wrong with us.*

This is hard because we don't want something to be wrong with us. We want to be "okay." We want to be normal and together and we don't want other people to judge us harshly. So we have a tendency to blame our problems on outside forces, other people, or bad luck.

We begin to see ourselves as victims, duped and deceived by forces beyond our control. We suspect we have somehow been singled out and specially targeted for woe. Now, this view of our fate poses an interesting paradox. Although we may suffer unbearable pangs of guilt and we chastise ourselves unmercifully for all of our mistakes, failures, and inadequacies, underneath all that self-blame is a deeply held, almost instinctive belief that we, ourselves, are in no way accountable for our troubles.

In our deepest heart of hearts, we believe utterly and truly that we are innocent of responsibility for our problems. We go around crying, "Look what's happened to me!" Self-pity becomes our constant companion.

This attitude is called the *victim stance,* and it's a major barrier to happiness. For, you see, as long as we consider ourselves to be victims, we remain incapable of doing anything to ease our plight.

We embrace the victim stance because, on either a conscious or unconscious level, it's important for us to preserve our need to be innocent of wrongdoing. This need to be blameless goes back to our early childhood days when we learned that misbehavior was usually followed by punishment.

Anyone who has raised children is acquainted with these familiar refrains:

"It's not my fault."

"I didn't do it."

"It wasn't me."

A child will often cling to these denials even when the evidence of his or her misbehavior is laying in broken pieces all over the floor. This doesn't mean the child is bad; it is merely one of the normal developmental stages all children go through.

The child's logic is simple. *I said I didn't do it, therefore, you shouldn't punish me. If you do punish me, you're the bad person, not me, and I have a right to feel bad because you treated me unfairly.*

THE VICTIM STANCE IN A NUTSHELL

I didn't do anything wrong. Somebody else did.

Therefore, I have a right to feel bad.

Some of us get stuck in this stage of development with unhappy results. Without conscious awareness, we believe accepting responsibility for our own lives is the same as admitting blame. And if we admit blame, something awful will happen to us. We will be punished, abandoned, rejected. So, in order to preserve our childish need to be innocent, we insist we are blameless and thus forfeit the possibility of help by denying any responsibility for our own lives.

The victim stance is especially destructive because few of us recognize it in ourselves. Oh, we hurl ugly accusations at ourselves and spend endless hours in self-castigation, but that is not the same thing as taking responsibility for our own behavior.

In order to conquer our depression, we must abandon the

victim stance. If we take responsibility for where our lives are, then new possibilities open up for us. We can take possession of the power and strength that lives inside each and every one of us. This may seem impossible because if we're very depressed, our energy is at a low ebb. It's hard to want to do anything positive when we're in a depressive daze. But the first step in getting out of depression is not so difficult. We start by being honest with ourselves.

Getting Beyond the Victim Stance

To get beyond the victim stance, *we must admit that our lives have become unmanageable.* Our despair is more than a passing bad mood. It's more than a normal reaction to disappointments, failures, and tragedies in our lives.

Let's face it — life is difficult. Not just for a few people, but for most of us. If this sounds grim, just take a few minutes to read the newspaper — accidents, disappointments, loss, pain, injustice, selfishness, cruelty, double-dealing, fraud, failure, and betrayal are detailed on nearly every page.

Yet, some people are able to maintain a healthy balance in the face of such adversity. These people do not like criticism, failure, and grief any more than the rest of us. But they know how to accept and handle it. They have no need to suffer in order to prove how unfair the world is. They seem to be made of sterner stuff than we are.

And perhaps they are made of sterner stuff. This doesn't mean they are somehow morally superior, but that the stuff they are made of — the genes, hormones, and nerve cells — is put together in a different package.

Individuals vary greatly in their ability to absorb stress and strain. Some people seem to be constitutionally better equipped to handle the slings and arrows of outrageous fortune. Others are plunged into severe depressive episodes when faced with even minor pressures, opposition, or loss.

Interestingly, nearly every study ever done on the subject shows that, in general, depressed people do not have lives that are any unluckier, more traumatic, or more tragic than do people who are not depressed. But depressed people react more negatively to disappointments than do other people.

So if there is little correlation between life circumstances and depression, what is the difference between them and us?

One major difference may be body chemistry.

Psychiatrist Nathan S. Kline, a recognized expert on the subject, describes depression this way:

> . . . it is a specific disorder, one that in most cases is very probably triggered by some disarray in the bio-chemical tides that sweep back and forth within the body . . . Within that context I regard depression as one of the most treatable of serious [illnesses].

Many other doctors and medical researchers are beginning to agree with Dr. Kline. The evidence is piling up and it indicates that most depressions are linked closely to mixed-up body chemicals.

How can this be?

The Hereditary Factor

Whoever first said "Life is not fair" certainly knew what he or she was talking about.

One of life's unfair acts is heredity. Some of us inherit genetic factors that make us tall or slim or with a lot of fast-twitch muscle fibers that give us a special edge if we want to become an athlete or a ballet dancer. We can also inherit genetic susceptibilities that aren't so desirable — factors that make us especially vulnerable to obesity, allergies, or diabetes, for example. It's all in the luck of the draw.

There is a growing body of scientific evidence showing that genetic factors play an important role in many forms of depression and alcoholism. And while depression and alcoholism are two separate and distinct conditions, they often go hand in hand.

So what does this mean for you?

It's quite simple. If you have close blood relatives who

have suffered from either depression or alcoholism, it is possible that you, too, have inherited genetic factors that make your nervous system susceptible to depression and alcoholism.

Think of it this way: Just as a diabetic's metabolism can overreact to ordinary foods, a depressive's nervous system can overreact to ordinary emotional stimulation. A couple of skipped meals, followed by a junk food binge can put a diabetic into a metabolic tailspin. And a couple of disappointments coupled with fatigue can ignite an emotional crisis in a susceptible depressive.

Studies done with children adopted at birth show fairly conclusively that the tendency toward depression is based on heredity, not on how you were raised. When children who had a biological parent who suffered from diagnosed depression were adopted into families with no history of depression, the adoptees were three times more likely to suffer from depression than the natural children of the adopting parents.

Of course, not everyone inherits the same genetic material. If you have a depressed parent, your sister may fall victim and you might not. The same goes for your children — just because you suffer from depression doesn't mean they will, too.

So, please: Don't waste your time blaming your parents for your depression and don't blame yourself if your kids have problems. None of us get to pick our genes.

The Biochemistry of the Blues

All of our thoughts and feelings, whether pleasurable or distressing, are controlled by biochemical reactions that occur in our brains and throughout our bodies. While our understanding of these processes is incomplete, it appears that an imbalance in brain chemicals can cause the mental, emotional, and physical symptoms of depression. So far, at least 50 different and distinct neurotransmitters (brain chemicals) have been identified by scientists, and an imbalance in even one of these important body elements can throw our mental system out of kilter.

We don't know exactly what causes an imbalance to occur, but a combination of hereditary factors, stress, and attitude may contribute.

What we do know is that many cases of depression can be effectively treated with antidepressant medications that change the biochemical balance in the brain. The most important point to remember is this: Hereditary susceptibility does not condemn us to a life sentence of the blues.

Consider this fact: With the help of medical care and positive life-style changes, people who have inherited a genetic vulnerability to a disease like diabetes can lead healthy, happy, and normal lives. The same is true for those of us who suffer from depression.

Some of us resist the idea that our distressing symptoms can be caused by something as unromantic as brain chemicals. We cling stubbornly to the belief that we are suffering from some mysterious and esoteric psychic burden that must be overcome by willpower and strength of character. But willpower and character don't have much effect on moods triggered by chronically messed-up biochemistry.

For this reason, medication is sometimes vitally important in your struggle for recovery.

Curtis, a man in his forties who possesses a truly sterling character, has suffered from mood swings ever since he was a teenager. And when I say mood swings, I mean that one day he could be happy as a lark and the next he would stumble off the end of the world into the emotional equivalent of the Le Brea Tar Pits. We are talking about a man suffocating in the deep black ooze of despair.

For years, Curtis dealt with his depressive episodes through willpower and strength of character. No matter how bad he felt, he hauled himself out of bed, showered, and headed for work where he fulfilled his obligations admirably. But, oh, how he suffered.

"I always told myself that all I had to do was suck up my guts and go on," Curtis said. "I kept going through sheer force of will."

Did it help end his depression?

"No," Curtis admitted, "I was just a depressed guy with a strong character and a will of iron."

But Curtis hasn't been seriously depressed in a couple of years now. What changed? His wife convinced him to see his family doctor, where Curtis laid out the whole story of his emotional suffering. After conducting a physical exam, the doctor prescribed an antidepressant medication that Curtis agreed to try. Within two weeks, he was showing signs of improvement. Within two and a half months, he was a new man. And he was chagrined.

He explained: "I had been struggling with this damn business of my black moods for 25 years. I couldn't believe how fast I improved after I started the medication. I could kick myself for waiting so long. And the truth is, if my wife hadn't insisted, I would never have made that doctor's appointment."

Curtis resisted the idea of taking medication because it didn't seem manly, and he was afraid he'd end up being dependent on the drug for life. He was surprised to find out that many patients don't need to take medication forever. Curtis was able to discontinue it after a little more than a year. And he's remained on a pretty even keel ever since.

"I know the medication helped straighten out my biochemistry," Curtis said. "But more important, it let me come out of my fog long enough to start looking at my life realistically. I realized I had to make some important changes in my attitudes. I worked on being more positive and less demanding. Now, when I have a setback of some kind at work or at home, I can handle it. I don't go off the deep end like I used to. I guess I've developed some pretty good coping skills I didn't have before."

Should You Consider Antidepressant Medication?

People suffering from depression can be divided into two groups:

Group One. Some people will swallow, eat, drink, or inject any substance that promises even temporary relief from emotional pain. People in this group usually need little convincing to get them to try antidepressant medications. Unfortunately, all of the other substances they are taking usually render the medication ineffective. And in combination with alcohol or street drugs, you can end up with a really dangerous concoction.

Group Two. Other people object to taking medication to combat their depressive feelings on the grounds of health, moral, or ethical reasons. People in this group tend to believe depression is a sign of moral failure or personal weakness. Needing medical treatment to alleviate mental and emotional suffering is considered a sign of personal failure, and even thinking about it causes considerable embarrassment. Concerns about side effects and worries about "needing a crutch" are also high on the list of objections to seeking medical assistance.

Whether you belong in Group One or Group Two or somewhere in-between, it is important for us to recognize that antidepressant medication is not *THE* solution to all our problems. But it can be part of the solution.

If you are stuck in a rotten situation or relationship, medicine won't suddenly make everything rosy and bright.

If you are abusing your body with alcohol and other drugs, tobacco or food, medication won't eliminate the bad effects of these substances.

If you habitually turn toward the dark, negative, and mean side of the human spirit, pills won't bring light into your world.

But if you are suffering from a medically treatable problem, if your body chemistry is seriously out of whack, a visit with a knowledgeable physician can set you on the right track. If you can get your body chemistry back in balance, you will be better able to deal with the very real problems we all face.

Now, just in case you're not convinced yet, let's look at some of the reasons why seeing a doctor can be the important first step in freeing youself from the bondage of bad biochemistry.

Chapter Four

Rx for Depression: See Your Physician

A psychologist friend of ours hasn't always been happy about the way doctors handled depressed patients in the past. "Too often they either prescribed sleeping pills or minor tranquilizers, medications that shouldn't be used by depressed people, or they ignored the depression altogether and said it's all in the head. Depressed people were treated like crocks or hypochondriacs."

But our psychologist friend has gained new respect for physicians in recent years. For one thing, doctors are more aware of the biochemistry of the blues. And they have more effective medications to combat depression.

Our friend told us, "I'm a psychologist. I have the right academic degrees, and I have many years of experience working with people who have various kinds of mental, emotional, and chemical dependency problems. I think I'm pretty good at helping people. But there are a lot of things I can't do for my clients. I can't diagnose a physical illness, do a blood test, or write a prescription. And sometimes, that's exactly what a depressed client needs. You simply can't imagine how difficult it sometimes is for me to persuade a depressed client that it is vitally important for them to see a doctor for a physical examination."

Why all the resistance? Partly denial, the fear of finding out something "really bad" is wrong. And part of the resistance comes from the inertia of depression itself which makes decisions seem unbearably hard. If you can't find a good reason to get out of bed, you probably won't be able to find a good reason to go to the doctor.

Our friend pointed out there may be other reasons for staying away from a doctor: "I've even been accused by a few clients of being in cahoots with the medical profession in order to gouge more money out of them. Which is interesting when you consider that for many years I worked in a public clinic which provided free services. But then, unreasonable suspiciousness is one symptom of depression."

Ending the Guesswork

The best reason for seeing a physician is to end the guesswork: "What's going on with me — am I crazy or something? Why do I feel so down? Why do I have to get hooked up to jumper cables to drag myself out of bed?" When you end the guesswork, you're in a much better position to take steps to effectively relieve the depression.

People often spend a great deal of time and money futilely seeking relief for depression through counseling and psychotherapy, when the depression stems from a medical condition. Although a medical examination may not determine the precise reason for your depression, it's extremely important to rule out physical problems that can mimic depression in either subtle or dramatic ways.

No amount of therapy will relieve a depression that is rooted in a physical disorder. For example, early explorers frequently suffered bouts of depression that were later discovered to be one of the symptoms of scurvy, a deficiency of vitamin C in the diet. In this case, desolation and melancholy could be relieved by eating citrus fruits, vegetables, and fresh meat.

Another form of diet-related depression occurred in cases

of pellagra, a common disease in southern states during the early part of the twentieth century. Pellagra victims were often suicidally depressed. One typical victim of this disease became so despondent that he filled his pockets with rocks and jumped into a well.

Pellagra was considered a mental illness for years before it was researched by the U.S. Public Health Service, which conclusively showed that pellagra resulted from a deficiency of vitamin B-3 (niacin), and it could be cured by providing patients with foods rich in niacin.

In more recent times, medical research has found many more physical disorders that carry depression as a major symptom. Infectious hepatitis and mononucleosis are two common illnesses notorious for making people feel depressed. The depression is real, but it is certainly not due to childhood deprivation or low self-esteem. The depression affects mental functioning, but it is not "all in the head."

A woman came to us very concerned about her son, Robert. Robert was in his late twenties, drove a truck for a living, and had always been an energetic and active person. For the past several months, he'd been listless, moody, and depressed. On at least two occasions, he'd unexpectedly burst into tears while talking to his mother. This shocked her because she hadn't seen Robert cry since he was ten years old. Something was terribly wrong, but Robert kept insisting he had no idea what it was. His mother suspected drugs, which Robert vehemently denied using.

We saw Robert a few days later and he didn't look good; his skin was pasty and the whites of his eyes had a yellowish cast. He told us that a couple of months previously he'd had a mild bug for a few days, but nothing serious. He hadn't even taken time off work, which he couldn't afford to do because he didn't get sick leave. He'd gone downhill emotionally ever since. As he talked, the tears started. He was terribly embarrassed by them, but he said lately he couldn't seem to help himself. The tears just came. We asked Robert to call his family doctor immediately and make an appointment, which he did.

As it turned out, Robert's mild bug had been hepatitis. Hepatitis can range from a mild infection without symptoms to one that is incapacitating. No specific medical treatment is available except a good diet and rest. Naturally, Robert neglected both as he lead-footed his 18-wheeler up and down Interstate 5.

While the hepatitis infection itself may last only a few weeks, the feelings of emotional and physical weakness can linger for months. Robert was fortunate. After just ten days of rest, he was well enough to go back to work.

Robert later said, "When the doctor told me I had hepatitis and explained the symptoms, I felt like an enormous burden had been lifted from my shoulders. For a while I really thought I was going crazy." Just knowing he had a physical disorder removed about 90 percent of Robert's worry and fears.

Another client named Betty echoed Robert's sentiment, although her health problem was not so easily solved. She had been ill for almost six years and had been called everything from lazy to crazy. Her husband thought she was a hypochondriac and her mother-in-law thought she had a weak character.

Betty felt low and she had a hard time remembering things. Some days she'd feel fine, but suddenly in the middle of doing something, she'd get so weak she could hardly walk. A couple of times she had to sit on the curb on a downtown street because her legs felt so shaky. When that happened, her mother-in-law called her a "guttersnipe."

"I felt like I had twenty-pound weights strapped to my wrists and ankles," she said. "I'd have headaches and joint-aches and swollen glands. My husband said I was imagining it all. After awhile I began to believe it, especially when my memory got so blurry. I was afraid I was losing my mind."

Betty participated in psychotherapy for several years. "Therapy helped me deal with my husband and his mother better and I think it helped me accept myself less judgmentally, but it never really helped my symptoms. I always felt tired and weak and useless. I thought I was the world's biggest neurotic."

During a routine physical exam with a new physician, the doctor asked Betty many probing questions. He also drew blood for tests. One of the tests he ordered was an EBV antibody level. EBV stands for Epstein-Barr Virus. This is the virus that causes infectious mononucleosis. When Betty returned for a follow-up visit, the doctor told her he thought she was suffering from Chronic Epstein-Barr Virus (CEBV). In plain English, she had chronic mono.

Most people who come down with mono have an acute illness, and then recover with no aftereffects. Others, and there may be thousands of them, develop a lingering illness that can produce a long-term, recurring, and debilitating disease. Symptoms include mood swings, bladder and digestive problems, strange sensations in the skin, and personality changes. Unfortunately, there are no specific medical treatments to combat CEBV. A healthy life-style that includes good nutrition, moderate exercise, rest, and stress management is probably the best way to go.

Because the symptoms of CEBV mimic neurosis and depression, sufferers are often given inappropriate treatment. "That was the worst part of it," Betty admitted. "I went into therapy and didn't get better. I spent so much time feeling guilty and sorry for myself I didn't have time for anything else. Getting the blood test and a diagnosis didn't make my physical symptoms go away, but I don't feel guilty anymore. I don't feel like a failure. And I can't tell you the big difference that one change has made in my life."

Infectious diseases aren't the only conditions that can trigger feelings of depression. Blood pressure pills, heart medicine, hormones, sedatives, and tranquilizers can cause severe mood changes. Some people also can be affected by birth control pills, antihistamines, or antibacterials. Now, this may be no big deal if you're taking a prescription for a week or so, but some individuals take a daily grab bag of medications for years.

Bruce, a lawyer in his late thirties, developed a mild case of high blood pressure for which his doctor prescribed medication. The pills brought his blood pressure under control as long as he took them daily. About a year later, Bruce sought counseling for what he called "a very personal problem." He'd lost his sex drive. He attributed this to a depression that he believed resulted from unresolved emotional conflicts buried deep in his unconscious mind during childhood. He felt apathetic, bored, and uninterested in his work and social life.

Before delving into his psyche, we advised Bruce to ask his doctor for a medication change. The doctor stopped the prescribed medication and decided to try treating Bruce's hypertension with diet and exercise. Within two weeks, Bruce was his old self again.

The symptoms of depression Bruce experienced were painful and real, but medically the problem wasn't difficult to treat. In a case like his, a minor change in medication may be all that's necessary. Bruce could have wasted years trying to uncover nonexistent emotional conflicts if he hadn't made a simple visit to the doctor.

An important note: Under no circumstances should you discontinue medication without first consulting your doctor. In the case of blood pressure or heart medicine, stopping medication on your own could be fatal.

When You Should Go to the Doctor

1. Are your symptoms unrelated to a recent trauma such as a death, job loss, or divorce?
2. Have your symptoms lasted for more than two weeks?
3. Have you had changes in your appetite, either eating too much or too little?

4. Are you experiencing sleep problems, either insomnia or wanting to sleep all the time?
5. Do you cry uncontrollably?
6. Have you been planning to commit suicide or to harm other people?

If you answered "yes" to two or more of these questions, or if you answered "yes" to the last question, now is the time to make an appointment with your doctor.

What Kind of Doctor Should You See?

A psychiatrist is a medical doctor who has special training in the diagnosis and treatment of mental and emotional disorders. Some psychiatrists practice medical treatment; that is, they physically examine their patients, take blood and urine tests, and prescribe medications. Others practice various kinds of talk therapy in much the same way a psychologist or counselor would.

When we think of getting treatment for a mental or emotional problem, a psychiatrist is usually the person we think of first. This is fine if you know one, or if you live in a metropolitan area where many psychiatrists practice. But what if you live in a small town or rural area? What if the process of finding a psychiatrist seems more than you can handle?

Today, many general practitioners and internists are on the cutting edge of diagnosing and treating depression in their patients. Why is this? One reason is that with the advent of effective antidepressant medications, the process of treating depression is being demystified. While your doctor probably has neither the training, time, nor inclination to provide you with psychotherapy, he or she may be qualified to diagnose, prescribe treatment, and monitor your recovery from depression. Ask your doctor if he or she has treated your kind of problem before and feels comfortable providing treatment. If the answer is "no," your doctor can probably refer you to a doctor who can treat you.

Some people feel reluctant to ask their regular physician for a referral to another doctor. They're afraid their doctor will be insulted or hurt by such a request. If your doctor is a true professional, this fear is groundless. Doctors make referrals all the time; it's a normal part of medical practice, and a good doctor knows when it's time to call in a specialist.

Now, what if you don't have a family doctor? What if you don't even know one? Now is the time to find one. Do you know anyone who has had a problem similar to yours? If they've been successfully treated, ask them about their doctor. A counselor or a therapist can often make a good referral and will frequently work closely with your physician to help monitor your progress.

Unless you're in the middle of a serious depressive or suicidal crisis, we'd suggest not using a hospital emergency room or an urgent care clinic for treatment of your depression. If medication is prescribed, you must be regularly monitored to make sure it's working correctly. Unless you're willing to return to the emergency clinic for regular follow-ups, it is not your best choice.

An important note: Listen, if it's three o'clock in the morning, you're at your wits end, and you're considering drinking all the household cleaners, an emergency care clinic is an excellent choice for treatment.

Another important note: What if the doctor you see is cold, rude, insensitive, and overbearing? What if you simply don't like the doctor?

Physicians, like the rest of humanity, come in a variety of personal styles, from Marcus Welby to Dr. Frankenstein. Some are incredibly competent medical specialists, but awkward and mechanical in dealing with patients. You need a physician you can both respect and trust, so you might have to seek out a new doctor who is both sensitive *and* competent.

Now a word of caution: Sometimes doctors tell us things we don't like or don't want to hear. When that happens, too many of us put a frozen smile on our face and leave, muttering to ourselves that the doctor is a quack and we'll never return. Don't let your false pride or hurt feelings interfere with your need for medical treatment. If your otherwise personable, kind, and skilled physician says something you don't like, do not — repeat: do not — discontinue treatment. When you quit treatment, it doesn't hurt your doctor — it hurts *you.*

What You Should Tell the Doctor

Prepare yourself for a shocking truth — *patients lie to their doctors.* Patients fib, minimize the truth, tell white lies and even whoppers. All the time. It seems totally absurd, but it's true.

Why would anyone do such a silly thing? Well, how does embarrassment sound as an excuse? Or shame or fear of being lectured?

You see, most of us know the difference between right and wrong. And most of us know the basics about how to live a healthy life-style. So, admitting to our doctor that we're smoking too much or drinking too much or lying awake at night crying or going two days without eating or eating tons of junk food, and generally behaving like self-destructive idiots *is* very embarrassing.

And perhaps there's another ingenuous thought running through the mind of the prevaricating patient: "If I don't tell the doctor the total truth about my life-style, maybe he'll find a more acceptable explanation for my condition." Some people would rather hear they have a tumor than be told they feel bad because they are drinking too much and eating in a unhealthy way.

So we lie to the doctor. We can't lie very effectively about smoking because the doctor can smell the stench of tobacco on our clothing and can see the nicotine stains on our fingers and teeth. But when the doctor asks, "How many packs do you smoke?" we might say: "I only smoke five cigarettes a day, I'm cutting down, I'm gonna quit, really Doc, I know it's bad for me." And five minutes after leaving the doctor's office we're halfway through our second pack of the day.

Or the doctor might ask, "How much do you drink?"

"Oh a couple of beers after work." (No need to tell him about last weekend when I got picked up for drunk driving. He doesn't want to know all that stuff, he just wants to find out if I'm an alcoholic. I'm not that bad yet.)

Men are especially stoic and defensive about anything that might be construed as an emotional problem. One woman told us that when her husband was depressed she finally persuaded him to see the family physician. "I don't think I can talk about this stuff," her husband confessed before the appointment. So she wrote a note to the doctor explaining in detail the problems her husband was having. "I know it seems childish," she says, "but it worked. With the help of that note, my husband was scrupulously honest with the doctor, and he got the help he needed. We all did."

Steve is a good example of someone who lied to his doctor out of embarrassment. Steve had been feeling low for several months, so he made an appointment for an exam. "I've got this feeling of pressure inside my belly," he told the doctor. "My liver hurts."

The doctor ordered blood tests and scans and x-rays. He couldn't find any abnormalities.

"How much do you drink, Steve?" he asked on a follow-up visit.

"Oh, the usual amount. A couple now and then, strictly social," Steve replied without a twitch.

"How's your diet?" the doctor asked.

"Fine," Steve said.

"Do you eat fruits and vegetables?"

"Yeah, of course. An apple a day," he joked feebly.

"How much coffee do you drink?"

"Couple cups."

"How about breakfast? Do you eat breakfast every day?"

"Oh, yeah."

"Good," the doctor sighed. "Sounds like your diet is okay."

Steve skulked out of the doctor's office feeling like a criminal. He had lied! He hadn't eaten anything green in weeks and he drank at least twenty cups of coffee a day and he ate breakfast every day if you considered a box of soda crackers and a bottle of wine at three o'clock in the afternoon to be breakfast.

Why did he do it? Why did Steve lie?

"Because I was embarrassed," he explains. "I'm an intelligent person, I've got a college education. I would've felt like a fool telling the doctor how I really lived. I mean, what kind of incompetent jerk lives on soda crackers and wine? I didn't want him to know I was that kind of jerk. It would be too humiliating."

Fortunately, Steve was so shocked by his lie that he immediately went to a bookstore and purchased several good books on nutrition, which he studied diligently. He also quit drinking.

"I realized that anyone who drank a fifth or more of wine a day and lied about it wasn't a social drinker. I don't know if I was an alcoholic, but I wasn't a social drinker. Social drinkers don't lie and cover-up. They don't need to drink to get through the day. I did, so I guess I had a problem. That was two years ago, and I haven't had a drink since. And, I'm pleased to say, my life is a lot better these days."

What about his aching liver?

"No problem," Steve laughs. "Hey, would I lie to you?"

Help Your Doctor Help You

The bottom line is this: Our doctors can only help us if we're honest, up-front, and truthful with him or her. In other words, in order to help yourself, you must help your doctor to understand what's going on with you.

We must move beyond our embarrassment and shame and tell the doctor exactly what's happening to us.

We must summon up the courage to say: "Doctor, I came

here today because I've been feeling very down lately. I think I'm depressed. I need some help." If you can't say it, write it out. Or have someone close to you talk to the doctor about your symptoms.

Furthermore, we must be willing to admit to how much we're drinking and what drugs we're taking — including prescriptions, over-the-counter medications, street drugs, and health store preparations.

And when the doctor asks you to describe your symptoms, do it. There is nothing you can confess or do or say that your doctor hasn't seen and heard before. You won't shock him. She won't think less of you.

If you are engaging in bizarre behavior such as burning yourself with cigarettes or nicking your arms with razor blades or forcing yourself to vomit ten times a day, you must believe me when I say you are neither the first nor the only person who has done these things.

The behaviors we are most ashamed of are
often the very ones we must own up to
if we are to recover.

Do you lay around the house unwashed and uncombed eating nothing but Sara Lee pound cake or Twinkies for days at a time?

Have you been so bogged down in despair that you're ignoring the needs of your children?

Do you cry uncontrollably?

Is your sex life a distant memory?

Do you feel life isn't worth living?

Is killing off a bottle of wine the only way you can get to sleep? (Or vodka. Or brandy. Or crème de menthe.)

Are you irritable and mean and abusive? Have you smashed dishes against the wall, kicked in the door, or ripped up your clothes?

Are you planning ways to kill yourself?

Do you feel like there's a dangerous monster inside you just waiting to get out?

For God's sake, tell the doctor so you can get some help. Don't let shame, guilt, and fear keep you trapped when it's so unnecessary. So what if admissions embarrass you? Embarrassment won't kill you; untreated depression just might.

A woman named Selma came to me for counseling because she was deeply depressed and considering suicide. But she didn't tell me that. Instead, she told me, "I want to get to know myself better. A friend of mine went into therapy and it really helped her grow into a more creative person. I want to explore some of the things that seem to be blocking my potential. You know, like sometimes I think I need to be more assertive. That sort of stuff."

What I didn't know was that Selma had come into therapy with a hidden agenda. Because of her feelings of shame and guilt, she didn't want to come out and say, "Hey, I've got a stash of 43 sleeping pills and I'm trying to work up the guts to swallow them all. My life is a mess and I need help or else."

She waited for me to ask the right questions, then she would dribble out her story, censoring the really bad parts, the black thoughts, the bitterness, hate, and rage. She didn't want to shock me, didn't want me to think she was a terrible person. So she evaded and lied and talked in circles.

But Selma's behavior is quite common. I've been guilty of it myself once or twice in my younger years. What about you? Have you ever been less than forthcoming with the truth when talking to a doctor or a minister or a counselor who was trying to help you?

Selma sincerely believed we could talk around her problems and, in some mysterious way, she could uncover and correct the causes of her despair without ever having to reveal to me how really awful she felt about her life and the future. Revealing her true self to another person seemed . . . so improper.

In our weekly sessions, Selma sat opposite me, sphinx-like

and inscrutable, waiting for me to ask the questions that would unravel the mystery of her feelings. Eventually, after many weeks, I did ask the right questions, and Selma's armor began to crumble. From there we made progress.

But what if I had remained dense? It's been known to happen. What if I had never asked the right questions? Or what if I'd accepted Selma's evasions and lies at face value?

Therapists and doctors are not mind readers. They are fallible human beings who can help us only as much as we are willing to help ourselves.

Since my experience with Selma, I have asked many people this question: "When you have gone to a doctor or therapist for help with a personal problem, have you ever lied or withheld information that was important to solving your problem?"

Almost everyone admits that, yes, they have been less than honest at times because they felt embarrassed or guilty or ashamed. Or they feared the doctor would order them to give up one of their favorite vices, like smoking, so they lied to protect their bad habit.

But a surprising number of people said they didn't offer important information about what was happening in their lives simply because the doctor or therapist didn't ask. Many patients seem to feel it's not their place to tell an important person like a doctor or therapist how to do their job. So they wait and wait for the questions that may never come.

As one person told me, "I just assumed you knew what you were doing. I thought it would be impertinent to offer my own thoughts or feelings if you didn't specifically ask me."

The message is this: *Don't assume your doctor or therapist will instinctively figure out what's wrong with you.* Don't wait for them to perform magic. Answer their questions honestly. And if they don't ask the right questions, tell them what's happening in your life. Give them a chance to help you.

Chapter Five

The Misery Mind-Set I

Bonnie's Story

Bonnie Mencke woke up at quarter to nine in the morning to the sound of her baby screaming and cartoons blaring from the television in the living room. She looked at the clock. Her husband had left for work over an hour ago.

She went to the bedroom door in her saggy nightgown, threw it open and yelled, "Can't you kids be quiet?"

The baby wailed louder.

Bonnie went into the living room where five-year-old Jason looked around from the cartoons he'd been watching. Six-week-old Kimberly lay on a quilt next to him. Her diaper was askew, but it looked clean — Jason's handiwork.

When she saw her kids, she felt dragged two ways at once. Her heart ached with love to see the brown curls and dark eyes that so closely matched her own; and at the same time a terrible, trembling rage swept through her, making her want to grab them by the shoulders and shake them until their brains rattled. Why couldn't they leave her alone? Why were they so needy and demanding all the time?

"Kimi's hungry," Jason said in a subdued voice.

Kimberly wailed.

Bonnie stood for a moment, glaring at them. Then she said, "Bring her here."

Bonnie collapsed on the sofa and opened the front of her nightgown as Jason struggled carefully with the weight of his little sister. He deposited her on his mother's lap and returned to his place in front of the television.

The baby's mouth found the breast and the crying ceased. Bonnie glanced across the room into the kitchen where dirty dishes filled the sink and spread out over the counter. A heap of soiled laundry spilled out of a basket onto the floor near the end of the sofa.

The work never ends, she thought. It wasn't like this when Jason was a baby. I could handle it then. Something is different now, there's something wrong with me. I'm a bad mother. I'm going to ruin my kids.

She thought of all the years of chores stacked up ahead of her like dirty dishes in a sink five miles deep, and the blackest despair she had ever known swept over her and carried her down. Her family was draining the life out of her.

Her husband's voice echoed in her mind. "Of course, it's harder with two little ones than it was with only Jason . . . stick with it, honey."

No, you stick it, she thought. Just leave me alone.

Kimi gurgled and fussed at the breast. Warmth — wet and sticky — seeped onto Bonnie's lap where the baby rested. The baby had emptied her bowels in the loose diaper.

Kimi began to howl. So did Bonnie. The sobs came from deep in her belly and shook her body; she could neither stop nor control them.

Jason looked up frightened. "Mommy?"

Bonnie couldn't respond. The sobs had closed off her throat. She was going to suffocate right there. She struggled for breath and a thought entered her mind. Maybe she would die. Yes, that would be good. It would look like a natural death. It would save everyone a lot of bother if she would just stop breathing and die.

Jason hustled over and took his little sister from his mother's arms. "Don't cry, Mommy," he said. "I'll fix it."

He changed his crying sister and set her back on the quilt, all the time watching his mother from the distance. She was huddled up in a ball on the couch, her tangled hair hanging down over her face. What was she doing? he wondered. Was she crying because he'd done something bad? "Mommy, I'm sorry," he said. He didn't know what he was sorry for, but it was sort of a good luck phrase that had worked in the past. He came to her and tried to put his arms around her. "I'll be good."

She pushed him away. "Leave me alone," she sobbed. "Mommy doesn't feel good."

"I better call Gramma, huh, Mommy?"

"No!" Bonnie screamed. She jumped up from the couch and ran into her bedroom, slamming the door behind her.

Frightened and alone, Jason picked up the phone and dialed the only phone number he knew.

Bonnie was in the middle of an acute depressive episode. After the birth of Kimberly, she had felt increasingly overwhelmed and unable to cope, and she couldn't understand why. She had wanted the new child; her delivery had been relatively easy, and the baby wasn't exceptionally fussy. Bonnie's husband, Paul, was attentive and supportive, and a cleaning lady came in twice a month to help with the heavy chores.

Still, as the weeks passed, Bonnie slipped further and further down into despair. It was like she was experiencing the most horrible pain imaginable; but the pain was not in her body. The pain was in her soul. She'd never felt anything like this before.

Little Jason's phone call brought Bonnie's mother running. She was shocked to see her daughter in such a state. Bonnie had always been a healthy, bright, and cheerful girl. The wretched, sobbing, dirty woman she found crouched in bed was like a stranger. Not knowing what else to do, Bonnie's mother called the doctor who had delivered Kimberly. He arranged for Bonnie to be admitted to the hospital for observation.

After five days of tests and consultations, she was released to go home. She was in better shape, but she was still deeply depressed. In the hospital, she'd been started on antidepressant medication which she continued at home. The doctors told her it would take at least two weeks for the medication to reach a level in the body where it "kicks in." They also told her she could expect a substantial improvement within four to eight weeks, with progress back to her normal mental state in subsequent weeks. In Bonnie's case, the doctors were right. Four months later, we met with Bonnie. It was hard to believe that such a short time ago this vibrant and smiling woman sitting across from us had been so depressed.

"I feel like my old self again," Bonnie said, holding Kimberly in her lap. "I still don't know what happened to me. It was like a black curtain wrapped itself around me and I couldn't fight my way out. It was really strange because I've always been a happy person and a positive thinker. But after Kimi's birth, I felt like a different woman. But I'm better now. I still regret that I had to give up breast-feeding Kimi, but what's important is that the medication helped me get back to normal."

Bonnie made an amazing recovery from a severe depressive episode. Within a few months, she was back to being a lively, happy, and healthy person capable of meeting her responsibilities and obligations with good cheer. She radiated enthusiasm and a positive outlook on life.

Was antidepressant medication responsible for these admirable qualities? No. Bonnie had always been a cheerful and positive person. After the birth of her second child, the accumulated effects of stress, fatigue, and hormonal changes created a biochemical fire storm in her body. The result was a devastating depression that might have gone on for months had her mother not forced her to seek medical care. A week in the hospital, followed up with appropriate medication, brought her biochemistry back into balance and restored her normal emotional equilibrium.

She didn't need counseling or long-term psychotherapy to develop a well-balanced personality. She had always had one, and after her biochemistry was returned to its normal state she was that way again. She was returned to her normal personality.

You might ask, "What is my 'normal' personality like?" If you are normally a bright, cheerful, generous, loving, and positive individual who has a biochemical imbalance in your body, appropriate medical treatment can return you to your normal, cheerful self.

But what happens to a person who is normally grouchy, self-centered, and negative? This kind of person can also be hit with a biochemical tempest that changes his or her normal negativity into a black, impenetrable despair. Will several months of antidepressant medication turn this kind of person into a cheerful, smiling, and happy philanthropist?

What do you think?

Misery as a Way of Life

Up until this point, we have discussed depression as a disorder caused by a mixed-up biochemistry. Now we're going to turn the corner and view depression from another angle.

Consider this: Our moods can be directly caused by the way we look at the world. If we have a positive attitude, we'll have positive feelings. If we're negative and pessimistic, our feelings will be dark and gloomy. In other words, our thoughts can create and control our feelings.

We know an aspiring actress named Mitzi who can be charming, but whenever things don't go her own way, she turns foul-tempered, moody, irritable, and plain miserable to be around. Recently she auditioned for a part in a play and flubbed one of the lines. A week later, Mitzi was still distraught.

"I made a fool of myself," she wailed, tears filling her eyes.

"I wish I were dead!" She sagged in her chair like a lifeless rag doll. "My life isn't worth living."

Just then the phone rang. It was the play's director. Mitzi had won the starring role. Suddenly the world brightened. Life was wonderful again and Mitzi danced off laughing and chirping with glee. "I knew I'd get the part. I just knew it!"

Anyone who had seen Mitzi ten minutes before the director's phone call would have felt justified in making a diagnosis of depression. But, although Mitzi frequently suffers from bad moods, sulkiness, unhappiness, and personal misery, she does not suffer from clinical depression. She is more like a young child who holds her breath and threatens to turn blue if she is not given her own way. Small disappointments enrage her. It's not fair, she thinks. I shouldn't be frustrated or denied. I deserve to get what I want.

It seems only natural to Mitzi to sulk when she is disappointed, to spiral down into one of her infamous dark moods. And, of course, it is natural for any of us to feel a momentary pang of unhappiness when we are faced with the obstacles of everyday life.

But many of us, like Mitzi, have elevated that amount of natural unhappiness into a way of life. *We possess what could be called a mind-set for misery.* We stubbornly cling to personal unhappiness and suffering. It's almost as if we've made suffering an essential ingredient of our personality. Indeed, unhappiness is an important part of our identity. As Carly Simon sang: "Suffering was the only thing that made me feel I was alive."

When this mind-set is part of our personality, we sincerely believe it's necessary, essential, and proper for us to suffer, moan, and sulk whenever we don't get what we want. We also believe we can only be happy if we obtain all of the achievements and rewards associated with the good life — money, looks, recognition, status, love, good sex, and the envy of every person who ever made us feel small, insignificant, or demeaned. Bluntly stated, we make ourselves miserable if we don't get what we perceive to be our share of the goodies.

Now listen, because this is important: If the misery mind-set is part of our personality, we're usually the last to know it. To us, it's so normal, natural, and deeply ingrained in our personalities that we don't recognize it in ourselves. To us, it's simply a way of life.

Is it possible that much of your misery is caused by your personal mind-set, rather than by whatever you've been blaming your problems on? Answer the following questions honestly.

1. Has your life been full of disappointments?
2. Have you been hurt deeply in the past and not gotten over it?
3. Is your whole life a struggle?
4. Do you often feel the people closest to you don't care enough about your feelings?
5. Have you been subjected to a lot of criticism and disapproval in your life?
6. Do you feel like a victim of bad circumstances?
7. Does it seem as if you have little or no control over the direction your life takes?
8. Are you convinced you are really incapable of improving your situation because outside factors are just too strong?
9. Have a lot of people you trusted betrayed you?
10. Is it important that you excel in all that you do?
11. Do you think your life would be a lot better if the people around you would just wake up and start acting right?
12. Does it seem like other people don't have to struggle as hard as you do to get what they want?

If you answered "yes" to five or more of these questions you are probably suffering from the misery mind-set. Every one of life's normal disappointments will wound you deeply. You will feel, either consciously or unconsciously, like a victim of circumstances out of your control.

This mind-set is not treatable with antidepressant medications because it is not caused by a mixed-up biochemistry. Anyone who has ever suffered from a biochemical depression knows that a phone call announcing good news will not bring about an immediate chemical balancing act.

But we believe *there is a relationship between the misery mind-set and an imbalanced biochemistry.* Our bodies and our brains do, after all, work together as one unit. When we tell ourselves life is awful, we should be miserable, and everything is black, our bodies will be most obliging in making these thoughts come true. In other words, we can think ourselves sick. Or, more remarkably, *we can think ourselves well.*

Gloom and Habitat: External Triggers For Depression

Depression, like many other illnesses, is a condition strongly influenced by outside factors — stress, the economy, the weather, marital strife, and so on. A number of studies have shown that life stresses may trigger depression in vulnerable people.

For example, there is a clear relationship between unemployment and suicide. The higher the unemployment rate, the higher the rate of attempted suicide. A person who is mildly depressed or who is vulnerable but not yet sick can be thrown into a complete depression by losing his or her job. But while unemployment is difficult for nearly everyone, only a small percentage of layed-off workers go off the deep end.

Usually, the people who react to misfortune by falling into despair possess the misery mind-set. The man or woman with the misery mind-set probably believes that without a job or a high income, they have no useful role in society. They feel defeated. They lose their sense of self-worth and purpose and lapse into depression.

Unemployment isn't the only outside factor that can leave

us feeling adrift and useless. Here are some other situations:

- The man or woman who has always been one half of a couple, but who becomes single due to divorce, death, or separation.
- The woman who devoted herself to children who are now grown up and out on their own.
- The jock who prided himself on his athletic prowess and ends up with bum knees and slipped discs, preventing him from maintaining a rugged life on which he based his manhood.
- The attractive woman who always turned heads on the street is suddenly 40 and fighting fat and wrinkles, and is called "ma'am" by the young men who used to find her desirable.

We might think that if these people become depressed in reaction to unpleasant circumstances, antidepressant medication should not have a positive effect on their symptoms. But that isn't the case. Many people who seem depressed in response to unpleasant external circumstances respond magnificently to antidepressants. Here's why:

The impact of unpleasant environmental events can be made worse by a person's negative attitudes. This can trigger a physical reaction in the human body called a *stress response*. The stress response can cause an imbalance in certain hormones and neurotransmitters, and this imbalance will then create a biochemical depression.

In simpler terms, here's a recipe for depression: Take one genetically vulnerable individual. Add a liberal amount of misery mind-set. Place in a stressful environment. Shake vigorously until the biochemistry is thoroughly mixed-up. Cover with denial and place in a dark corner until sour. Serve with generous portions of guilt, anger, and self-loathing. Guaranteed to make life joyless.

Breaking the Depression Chain

This recipe for depression can be seen as an interlocked chain which includes environmental, attitudinal, and genetic factors. We can defeat depression by breaking into this chain at any point.

1. We can work toward eliminating environmental stress.
2. We can work toward developing a more positive mental outlook.
3. We can compensate for genetic vulnerability with positive life-style changes and medical treatment.

The approach that we have seen as most effective in helping people to permanently overcome depression combines all three of these factors. We've already discussed the importance of antidepressant medications. Now, let's focus our attention on changing the misery mind-set.

Chapter Six

The Misery Mind-Set II

The misery mind-set is caused by mixed-up thinking, beliefs, and values. What are some of these mixed-up beliefs?

- I must always get what I want.
- I must always be the best.
- It's terrible if I make a mistake.
- The people I love must always love me back.
- I can't stand it if someone is mean to me.
- I ought to think only good thoughts.
- I shouldn't have bad feelings.
- People who do something wrong deserve to be punished.
- People should recognize and appreciate all the good things I do.
- I shouldn't fail.
- If I have a hard time in my life, it means there's something wrong with me.
- If someone really cares about me, they shouldn't do things that hurt my feelings.
- Getting what I want shouldn't be hard.
- If I can't be the best, then I don't want to be anything.
- I shouldn't have to put up with hassles, irritations, pain, or annoyances.

These beliefs are all irrational because they are not based on reality. In the real world, life is hard. We make mistakes. We fail. We face a hundred annoying hassles every day. People are sometimes mean to us for no good reason. Sometimes we are the ones who behave badly. This is life.

And here is a distressing fact of life many of us seem to have never learned: *We can't always get what we want.*

But a lot of us go around in a brown fog half the time because we cling to the irrational belief that life holds only two possibilities for us.

Possibility #1: We must get what we want, when we want it, because we want it.

Or . . .

Possibility #2: Failing in Possibility #1, we must be miserable.

We insist that if the universe doesn't run according to our specifications, we must hold our breath and turn blue.

Sonia is a good example of someone who possesses the misery mind-set. Sonia's misery mind-set is interesting because she has also suffered from a true biochemical depression which was relieved through proper medical treatment.

Sonia could best be described as what one former politician called a "nattering nabob of negativism." Although she was attractive, intelligent, and had a good sense of humor when the joke was on the next guy, Sonia, who wanted so desperately to be liked, drove the people close to her away with her complaints about the awful things that kept happening to her. At work or at play, she found a way to turn every conversation around to her own troubles and woes. In short, the woman was a pain.

When she was in her mid-40s her normal negativity turned into something darker: a deep depression that left her gaunt, sleepless, and contemplating suicide. She consulted a psychiatrist and was started on antidepressant medications.

Those of us who knew her were filled with hope. Perhaps Sonia could now reach the potential we all recognized in her. If only she could be freed from her negative outlook on life, all of us — not just Sonia — would have a happier existence.

The medication worked. In a matter of a few short months,

Sonia had regained her appetite and her health. She slept soundly at night, and fantasies of death no longer haunted her.

Yet, despite her renewed lease on life, she was still one of the most sullen, bitter, angry, cynical, self-absorbed, and demanding people we knew. Still miserable, but no longer biochemically imbalanced.

Sonia was not able to find a measure of inner peace and contentment until she started working to modify the irrational and negative thought patterns that made her so miserable and miserable to be around.

What about you? Is it possible that a negative, bitter, irrational, and demanding outlook on life could be poisoning your whole existence? More important, is it possible to change blue moods into a brighter outlook by positive thinking?

How Thoughts Control Your Feelings

Before we go further, let's define what we mean by thoughts. The technical word for thoughts is *cognitions.*

Cognitions are the perceptions, attitudes, and beliefs which determine the way we look at things. Our emotions, both pleasant and distressing, will be determined by the way we perceive and interpret what's going on around us. This is a simple neurological fact. We cannot physically or emotionally respond to an event until we perceive it and process it in our minds.

Once a perception occurs, however, a complex chain of events take place inside our bodies.

- Our autonomic nervous system responds.
- Hormones and other body chemicals are released into our system.
- The resulting biochemical changes in our bodies are interpreted either as physical symptoms or as emotions, or both.

So, our emotions are created in a process like this:

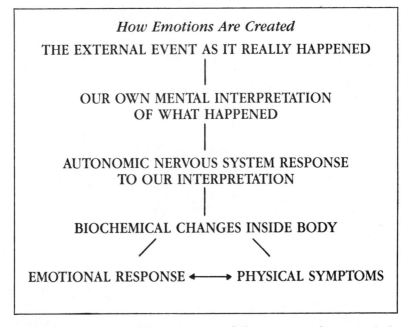

How Emotions Are Created

THE EXTERNAL EVENT AS IT REALLY HAPPENED

OUR OWN MENTAL INTERPRETATION
OF WHAT HAPPENED

AUTONOMIC NERVOUS SYSTEM RESPONSE
TO OUR INTERPRETATION

BIOCHEMICAL CHANGES INSIDE BODY

EMOTIONAL RESPONSE ⟷ PHYSICAL SYMPTOMS

We're usually totally unaware of this process because it is automatic and can happen in a split second. For instance:

1. You are crossing a street and you see a car coming at you (real event and perception).
2. Your mind signals DANGER! Get out of the way or die (mental interpretation).
3. Your body releases adrenaline and other hormones (nervous system response and biochemical changes).
4. Half scared out of your wits, you jump back to the curb with your heart hammering in your chest (emotional and physical response).

If for any reason, your mind doesn't interpret the car racing at you as a dangerous or negative event, you won't feel frightened. Or if you see a harmless parked car and perceive it as rolling toward you, you will respond as if you're in real danger, even though you're perfectly safe.

In other words, *it's not what happens to us that determines how we feel, it's how we interpret what happens that counts.*

One of us dramatically experienced this phenomenon first-hand about twenty years ago. I (Gayle) was a college student working a summer job in Alaska. I was a totally inexperienced flyer. My jet flight from Seattle to Fairbanks was my first plane trip; to me, it was about as exciting as riding on a bus. But on my first flight in a small four-seater airplane, we crashed about five minutes after takeoff.

The plane was in trouble from the start, but I didn't know it. I remember thinking to myself, these small planes sure do ride rough, don't they? Since I figured the pilot knew what he was doing, I entertained myself by watching the scenery roll by. As a brick schoolhouse came into view, I calmly thought to myself, gee, I think we should be flying a little higher. About 30 seconds later, we crashed. Luckily, all injuries were relatively minor.

During this entire process I wasn't one bit frightened, and it wasn't because I'm an exceptionally strong and courageous person. My mind simply wasn't interpreting the bumpy ride as dangerous. The pilot and the other two passengers admitted they had been scared stiff; they assumed I had been too. They couldn't get over how bravely the little city girl acted during the whole ordeal.

"Can you believe it?" they told people admiringly. "That little college girl didn't scream once. Cool as a cucumber, she was."

What they didn't know was that later that night when I had a chance to sit down alone and fully think about the implications of what might have happened, I fell apart. This is another step in the process of human emotional response. It's called *reinterpretation*, and it's something we all do. My reinterpretation went like this: I thought, my God, we crashed. I could have been killed. I could have been incinerated or mangled or maimed for life. I imagined my grief-stricken parents weeping at my funeral. I even pictured my corpse in the ground being eaten by worms.

I really worked myself into a state! I shook and cried for an hour and the next time I had to fly, my first thought was, Ack! Ack! A flying death machine! It's not hard to figure out what my emotional and physical reactions were like.

Now, in all honesty, I have to admit that my emotional response (anxiety, weeping, shaking, pronounced fear of future flying) was not determined by the reality of the plane crash.

This was reality: (a) during the five minutes before the crash, I was unaware we were in trouble and I felt no fear or unease; (b) the actual crash happened quickly and although the plane was totally destroyed, the passengers were not; (c) all the terrible things that could have happened, did not.

All my distressing emotional symptoms were caused by my later cognitions about the crash. My reinterpreted cognitions included: (a) negative thoughts (I could have been killed!); (b) visualizations (weeping parents, a wormy corpse); (c) fantasies about alternate outcomes (What if I had ended up in a wheelchair? What if my face had been scarred?); (d) and a belief that because something bad (crashing) had happened to me, I was supposed to be upset.

My negative emotions were caused by my negative cognitions which were a distortion of reality.

My thoughts and feelings seemed perfectly valid to me although they were not based on what had really happened to me.

Now, listen, because this next point is of enormous importance for anyone who wants to recover from the hell of mental depression:

Behavioral research clearly documents that the negative cognitions which cause our negative and distressing symptoms are almost always based on distortions of reality. Our beliefs are often irrational, our thoughts twisted, and our attitudes plain wrong. We dwell on the negative and ignore the positive. *And sometimes we make up memories of things that never really happened in order to justify our bad feelings.*

Yes, that's right! Almost all depressed people brood and fantasize so much about being abandoned, unloved, unwanted, rejected, ridiculed, or betrayed that we begin to incorporate our fantasies about unpleasant happenings into our memories of real events. This doesn't mean we've lost touch with reality; it's simply a sign that our thinking has become disordered and distorted.

A 30-year-old electronics technician named Bobby was being treated for depression and addiction at a well-known clinic. Part of his treatment involved therapy sessions with his entire family, including his parents and his older sister. During one session, Bobby turned on his sister, Leona. "I trusted you," he hissed. "And you betrayed me."

Leona was speechless, for she had no idea what Bobby meant.

"Remember that time when I was in the eighth grade and got picked up for stealing hubcaps?" Bobby asked.

Leona shook her head.

"No, of course not," Bobby responded sarcastically. "I had to spend the night in jail. You could've gotten me out if you wanted to."

"Bobby," his mother interrupted. "You only spent a couple hours in jail. You were released to my custody around three o'clock in the morning. I don't understand why you're mad at Leona."

"Because of what she said to me when you guys came to pick me up," Bobby said. "I felt really terrible and I was hoping my sister would have a little sympathy and understanding for what I'd been through." He turned to Leona, looking her straight in the eyes. "I'll never forget what you said to me. You told me you were ashamed of me, that you'd rather not have a brother at all than one who was a thief. All I did was take a five dollar hubcap and you ripped me up one side and down the other. You treated me like I was dirt. I've never been the same since. When the person you love and trust the most betrays you like that, you just don't ever get over it."

"Bobby," Leona said in total bafflement, "I don't know what you're talking about. When you were in the eighth grade, I'd already left home. I was living clear across the country. This is the first I've ever heard about you being arrested."

"Oh, sure," Bobby responded in disgust. "Another lie."

"Leona is telling the truth," their mother said. "I picked you up at the station. Leona was in New York. I never told her you'd been arrested. What you're saying never happened."

"But I remember the whole thing," Bobby insisted.

"You're mistaken," Leona said. "I'm sorry if you've been feeling bad about this for all these years, but you're all mixed up. *I was not there.*"

In reality, Leona had not been there when her brother had been arrested and released from jail. But in the abstract world of Bobby's private thoughts, Leona's presence had loomed large.

When fourteen-year-old Bobby had been arrested for petty larceny, he had suffered deep feelings of guilt, shame, and embarrassment. Of grave concern to him was what his beloved older sister would think of his misconduct. Would she reject him? Ridicule him? Hate him? As he sat in the jail cell, he imagined various scenarios of how she would react to the terrible news. He thought up excuses, rebuttals, and rationalizations that he might use in responding to her disapproval.

Later at home, when his father yelled at him, then gave him a whipping with a leather belt, Bobby kept thinking to himself; if Leona was here, she wouldn't let him hurt me like this. And, indeed, Leona had always intervened in her younger brother's behalf.

But Leona was in New York.

Bobby took his whipping and went to his room to sulk. He

spent a lot of time in his room over the next few months because his father grounded him until his fifteenth birthday. In his mind, Bobby relived his humiliation and pain over and over again, and slowly, as time passed, his memory of the actual events became blurred with memories of his fears about what Leona would think of him and his anger toward her for not rescuing him from his father's wrath.

At fourteen, Bobby could remember that Leona had not helped him because she was in New York. In his adult life, he only remembered that she had not helped him. He reinvented the facts of the situation to justify his feelings of abandonment, rejection, and betrayal. His sister became an enemy in his fantasies — unfair, cruel, and not to be trusted. Bobby then told himself he had a right to be depressed because no one really loved him.

Bobby's thinking was clearly distorted and just plain wrong; consequently, his emotions were distorted.

It would be easy to dismiss Bobby as an oddball, a rare bird with really messed-up thinking patterns.

In fact, Bobby's mental gyrations are quite common. We've all twisted and reinterpreted certain memories, and not always in a negative way. I know a woman who suffered through an abusive relationship for several years. Now that the affair is over, she waxes eloquent over how wonderful it all was. She has twisted the ugly truth into a beautiful memory and has just about convinced herself to reconcile with the brute.

We can reinterpret the past in nearly any way we choose; unfortunately, our depressive tendency is to twist it into a shape that harms us.

When we possess a misery mind-set, or when, like Bobby, we take the victim stance, we perceive the world as dark, gloomy, and unfair regardless of what it is really like. We believe life is really as bad as we imagine it to be. We begin to reinterpret the past to conform with our negative frame of mind, and when we think about the future we imagine all the terrible hurts, betrayals, and rejections that could possibly ever occur.

All these dark interpretations affect our autonomic nervous system which reacts by flooding our bodies with a whole array of biochemical juices, triggering the emotional and physical responses that best match our mental interpretation of what's going on around us.

In other words, we think ourselves sick. We must understand this process completely, because we can turn it around and use it to think ourselves well.

Chapter Seven

Singing the Blues

Kay's Story

"Look at me," Kay said, kneading her hands over her heavy thighs. "Who could ever love someone who looked like me? I'm a total screw-up. I can't do anything right. No one cares about me."

Kay's sad feelings overwhelmed her. She felt alone and unloved even though she visited her parents regularly, had a boyfriend, and a close friendship with Lori, a woman she'd known from high school. When Kay told Lori about these feelings of loneliness, Lori was perplexed. She asked, "What about Aaron? I know he's devoted to you. What about your marriage plans?"

Kay sighed. "Yes," she said, "but . . ." She shrugged forlornly, fought off a catch in her voice, and the tears came. "He says he loves me," she admitted, "but he doesn't make me *feel* loved."

The important people in Kay's life really did care about her. But they were beginning to find her continual need for reassurance and her subtle demands for undivided attention draining.

"Kay's my best friend," Lori told me later, "but I can't arrange my life around her needs. If I make plans with another friend, Kay's feelings get hurt. No matter how much attention I give her, it never seems like enough. She always wants proof that I'm her friend. I feel like I'm being smothered and our friendship's getting to be a burden. I don't know what more I can do to convince her that I care about her. And, to be honest, I'm getting tired of trying."

Kay was an intelligent and sensitive young woman, and she immediately sensed her friend pulling away from her. While this realization hurt Kay's feelings, it didn't surprise her. She'd been expecting it all along. Kay saw Lori's behavior as just more proof of Kay's own unworthiness. It was added evidence to what she already felt to be true: she would never be happy.

Lonely, unhappy, and sliding in and out of periods of deep depression, Kay's thinking became indelibly stained by her moods. And her perception about her life and her relationships became distorted. Kay began to see herself as a perpetual victim of ingratitude, unkindness, and betrayal on the part of her loved ones. With uncanny precision, she could detect the insincerity of others in seemingly harmless casual remarks. She dignified this ability by calling it her "built-in crap detector." At times she could see she was being unfair to her friends, but still, the bad feelings were so convincing.

Many people who have periods of depression or who are continually unhappy and dissatisfied begin to feel like aggrieved victims, as if there's a conspiracy to make their lives more difficult. Self-doubt becomes a model for their view of the world and sets the stage for an attitude of distrust.

Do you know someone like this? Do you perhaps recognize these characteristics in yourself? Do the following statements describe your attitudes?

1. I have found other people will usually take advantage of me if I give them a chance.
2. People I have trusted in the past have disappointed me, let me down, or hurt me on many different occasions.
3. I keep hoping the people I care about will treat me right, but usually they end up doing something that hurts me.

4. I don't like to talk about it, but I have been rejected and betrayed many times.
5. I believe if I'm nice to people, they should be nice to me in return.
6. People don't understand me very well, and they don't really try to understand.
7. I have been hurt by two-faced people a lot.
8. I think people would be surprised — even shocked — if they knew what I was really like inside.

Did you answer "yes" to four or more of these questions? If you did, you have undoubtedly suffered much pain and anguish in your life. You have probably tried again and again to win the love, admiration, and friendship you so desperately desire, but problems keep getting in the way. You may feel so hurt and so burned by life that you're no longer willing to reach out for new relationships. "Who needs it?" you might say to yourself. "Who needs that kind of pain?"

When a person has suffered like this, he or she is likely to respond in one of two ways.

1. *Emotional isolation.* We cut ourselves off from other people almost completely. We may have polite interactions with neighbors, co-workers, or store clerks; we might even be considered charming and friendly by the people we come into contact with daily; yet we are essentially alone and cut off from human relationships.
2. *Superficial intimacy.* We may engage in romances and friendships that appear to be close, but beneath our warmth we're constantly on guard, protecting ourselves, and remaining invulnerable. We feel our friends don't really know us. Our romances may be based mainly on sex because that's the only way we know how to relate to another person. Our emotions are hidden, and we're constantly looking for signs that our friends or lovers are going to abandon us. This makes us defensive, fearful, or angry.

The Injustice Collectors

All of us, at some time in our lives, have been ill-treated, jilted, hurt, or betrayed. We don't know anyone who has had the good fortune to escape emotional pain. Occasional hurt feelings are a natural part of living. But it's not natural to suffer continual hurt and emotional pain. One of the most common perceptions shared by depressed people, however, is that their lives are, always have been, and always will be filled with pain.

We're going to say something now that may shock and offend you. It is something none of us wants to hear said about ourselves, yet it is a truth we must face if we are to change our lives in a way which enables us to escape from our loneliness and depression.

Consider this: When, by our own reckoning, we are universally mistreated by the people we live with, work with, or love, the likelihood is that the problem exists within ourselves.

- We may think of small infractions by loved ones as major crimes against us.
- We may imagine injuries which in fact we have not suffered.
- We may behave in a way that arouses the anger of the people around us.
- We may place ourselves in destructive situations, and then lack the fortitude to free ourselves.

Or, like Kay, we may engage in all of these behaviors.

Kay became an *injustice collector*. She kept a list in her mind of every wrong and every hurt she had suffered. She interpreted the words and actions of her friends and loved ones in the most negative way. Whenever she was feeling down, she rummaged around in her mind, found memories of past injustices, and used them to reinforce her new worries and concerns. Sometimes it seemed as if she actually looked for situations that had little likelihood of a positive outcome.

For example, if her friend, Lori, didn't call as expected, Kay thought to herself, yeah, she doesn't have time for me any-more. This is just like the time another friend dumped on me.

These thoughts — based on fantasy, not reality — created in Kay feelings of rejection, sadness, and betrayal. When Lori finally did call, Kay would be sulky and uncommunicative, defensive of her hurt feelings, and antagonistic toward her friend. Lori, who had no way of knowing about Kay's inner dialogue, was baffled. What was wrong this time? As Kay's defensiveness increased, Lori found herself pulling away. The friendship was becoming too difficult.

Kay had created a vicious circle of loneliness. Because she feared abandonment by the people she loved, she interpreted their words and behaviors in a negative way; and because of her negative thoughts and feelings, she reacted in a defensive and antagonistic way toward the people who loved her; and because she was so defensive and emotionally demanding toward them, they became angry and rejecting toward her. Kay feared abandonment. Her reaction? She sulked and acted grouchy if people didn't treat her just right. And because she acted grouchy, she was in danger of being abandoned. The circle was complete. Her worst fears were coming true be-cause she was behaving in a way that almost guaranteed they would. She had created what is called a *self-fulfilling proph-ecy*. When she found evidence supporting her prophecy, she felt justified in saying, "See, I was right. I am being mis-treated, and that's why I feel bad."

Most of the time Kay, just like the rest of us, was not con-sciously aware of the thoughts that caused her depression. All she knew was that she felt alone, used, and unloved. The logic that created Kay's feelings was simple. She told herself, "I feel unlovable, therefore I am unloved." This kind of logic is called *emotional reasoning,* and it is an important factor in almost all depressions. Because we feel so bad about our-selves and our lives, and because our bad feelings are so powerful and so real, we assume our feelings are based on facts. Emotional reasoning is destructive because our negative emotions are frequently based on distorted thinking. The following irrational beliefs occurred in Kay.

- If my parents really loved me they would have paid my way through college.
- If my best girlfriend really cared about me she wouldn't spend time with other people when I need her to keep me company.
- If my boyfriend found me attractive he wouldn't make me feel bad by looking at pictures of pinup girls with gorgeous, skinny figures.
- I'm twenty pounds too heavy, and fat girls are unworthy, unlovable, and unattractive.

Kay spent much of her time singing the blues. She kept telling herself her excess weight diminished her value as both a woman and a human being. She then set about finding evidence to confirm this strong belief in her basic unworthiness. Of course, after examining the actions of her parents, friend, and fiance under a microscope every day, she found the evidence she was looking for. But, in reality, her feelings of being unworthy, unloved, and rejected were without validity.

Why? Because her basic premise — fat girls are unworthy — is irrational and has no valid basis in fact.

Fat Girls Don't Have Fun: A Weighty Challenge

Recognizing our irrational beliefs and giving them up is difficult because they are reinforced by our family, the culture we live in, and by the media messages that surround us.

Ads for one-calorie sugar-free soft drinks feature attractive women frolicking in skimpy bikinis. The message is: "Drink Skinny Soda and you, too, can have fun and be a worthy person with a trim body men will find irresistible."

Magazine ads for glamorous clothes and cosmetics show models who are both thin and well-developed with firm muscles and large bosoms. Every night on television we see commercials with shapley women who love low calorie diets and heavy-duty aerobic workouts. "You too can be a size six and love it," the ads seem to say. "All you need is willpower and get-up-and-go." A stirring message to those of us whose willpower got up and went to the refrigerator five minutes ago. Is it any wonder that to many of us the idea that over-weight women are less worthy than thin women seems perfectly logical and realistic?

Let's put this irrational belief into perspective by looking at some similar beliefs that were accepted without question in the past.

- Black people are unworthy.
- Jewish people are unworthy.
- Women are less worthy than men.
- Italians are less worthy than WASPs.
- The only good Indian is a dead Indian.

These prejudices have been challenged so much in recent decades that nowadays we consider people who embrace these falsehoods to be bigots and chauvinists.

Yet, Kay saw nothing irrational or false in her belief that fat girls are unworthy and unlovable. Even her definition of "fat" was irrational. As little as ten pounds above ideal fashion model slimness brought on self-condemnations and self-labeling with terms like "blimp" and "hog."

Sometimes I Feel Like a Motherless Child

By clinging to the belief that her worth and her weight were bound together, Kay perpetuated her feelings of depression. In the words of the blues classic, she felt like a motherless child — abandoned, worthless, and alone.

Kay, like all depressed people, kept her negative feelings alive by a constant inner flow of negative self-talk. If her boyfriend was momentarily critical or inattentive toward her, the following thoughts flew through her mind: I'm a failure. No one will ever love me. I should be prettier, then he wouldn't treat me this way. I can't stand it. He's such a jerk to make me feel like this. I try to do everything just the way he wants it, and this is what I get! I hate it. I'd be better off dead.

It was like she had a fiendish little disc jockey in her head who kept up a steady stream of self-hate jabber between playing records like "Unlovable Me" and "Forever Sad and Blue" from the Top 40 Melancholy Golden Oldies.

Negative emotions are always preceded by negative thoughts or negative self-talk. Because our negative self-talk is automatic and can take place in a split second, we are usually unaware of it.

Recovery from depression depends in large part on becoming aware of our negative self-talk and learning to substitute positive self-talk in its place.

Who's Really Saying All Those Terrible Things?

Most people are probably about 95 percent unaware of their negative thoughts and self-talk. We focus on the bad feelings and physical symptoms that overwhelm us — a fast beating heart, a tightness in the stomach, sweating, a sense we can't breathe right, tingling, fear, sadness, guilt, forebodings of doom, or expectations of disaster.

You may have tried different ways to control these terrible feelings, but they keep coming back. The reason the bad feelings keep coming back is because you haven't challenged the depressing and negative inner dialogue going on in your mind. Who's really saying all those terrible things? You are. Over and over and over again. If you become aware of the negative self-talk that causes your bad feelings, you can begin to control unpleasant emotions and change them into something more positive.

Kay was totally unaware of the negative thoughts racing through her mind. Until she entered therapy, she challenged her feelings of worthlessness with a string of unsuccessful diets. Not surprisingly, each dieting failure increased her burden of self-loathing. It had never occurred to her to challenge the validity of her basic premises (that she was unworthy, and that she deserved to be treated badly) or the accuracy of the perceptions she used to create such feelings.

She had spent most of her life believing that if she felt something, the feeling was based on true events. Her motto could be described as, "I feel unworthy, therefore I am unworthy." It would be far more accurate for us to say, "I am a thinking, feeling person, and I do not have to feel unworthy and miserable."

Rejecting False Beliefs

Just because we believe something doesn't make it true. If we put all of our energy into believing elephants can sprout wings and fly, it will not make this false belief true. If a thousand other people confirm this belief by saying, "Yes, indeed, I believe it, too. Why, my daddy and granddaddy told me about flying elephants, and just yesterday I heard one flapping its wings outside my window," . . . well, all the belief in the world won't make flying elephants a fact.

And just because your father used to say every week, "You're never going to amount to anything!" — just because he said it, it doesn't make it true.

If a woman's parents taught her a female's body was unclean and a source of sin and shame — just because they said it, it doesn't make it true.

If a man's school teachers had told him he was unruly and would never be able to hold a job — just because they said it, it doesn't make it true.

All the fashion magazines told Kay she was undesirable as a woman because she wore a size 16 — just because they said it, it doesn't make it true.

During the sensitive, vulnerable years of childhood and adolescence we are barraged with dozens of negative messages which shame us, embarrass us, and make us believe we are unworthy.

Now listen: Just because we hear a negative message that says we are unworthy, bad, or inadequate, it doesn't mean we have to listen to it. Just because somebody else believes something bad about us, it doesn't make it true. We don't need to live up or down to other people's false beliefs about who or what we are. If a thousand people tell you that elephants fly and, oh, by the way, you're unworthy because you're short . . . you don't have to listen.

Rejecting Negative Messages

Try this exercise: Get a piece of paper and a pencil. At the top of the sheet, write the false belief or negative message you wish to reject. Read the message out loud. Then fill the page with these words: I REJECT THIS BELIEF. Write it and say it out loud over and over again. For example:

Negative Message: *I must always be perfect.*
I REJECT THIS BELIEF
I REJECT THIS BELIEF
I REJECT THIS BELIEF
I REJECT THIS BELIEF
Negative Message: *I'm no damn good.*
I REJECT THIS BELIEF
I REJECT THIS BELIEF
I REJECT THIS BELIEF
I REJECT THIS BELIEF

Some false beliefs are easily given up; others will require much time before we can truly convince ourselves to stop listening to the hurtful, false messages that have reinforced our bad feelings about ourselves.

Attitude Conditioners

Here's another confidence-producing exercise. We need to practice this exercise with the idea that we're about to change our attitudes. We're going to get rid of all those old, draining, negative thoughts; in their place we're going to substitute thoughts of hope and inspiration.

Every day for the next week, take a few minutes to memorize a new attitude. Throughout the day, refer to the new positive thought until it is thoroughly implanted in your mind. On each subsequent day, memorize a new attitude and add it to the others. Repeat the attitudes each day, allowing them to replace old, automatic, negative thoughts.

Here's an example:

Day 1: I feel myself growing stronger and more healthy every day.

Day 2: I feel a new depth, a new dimension, and a new aura of happiness growing inside me.

Day 3: I feel in tune with all existence. I am complete and whole. I am falling into rhythm with God.

Day 4: I feel myself surrendering to happiness and in that surrender is power.

Day 5: I feel myself saying, "Yes." "Yes" to life, "yes" to hope, "yes" to love. Every fiber of my being is saying "yes" to happiness.

Day 6: I feel alert and aware today. I am centered, grounded. I feel laughter and happiness alive inside me.

Day 7: Today I will sing a song, tell a joke, give a compliment. I will give whatever I can give, for it costs me little and brings me an abundance of joy.

We can saturate our minds and fill our hearts with hope. Faithful practice can produce astonishing results.

Chapter Eight

Challenge Your Depression

The next time you find yourself sinking into a depressive state, STOP! Take a deep breath. Okay, now pause a moment to analyze and acknowledge what's going on. You are experiencing certain emotions. What are they? Anger? Fear? Guilt? Dread? Hate? Hopelessness?

Don't just say, "I'm depressed." That's shorthand for a whole constellation of distressing thoughts and feelings making up the complex condition we call depression.

Ask yourself this specific question: *What am I feeling?* Stopping for a minute to sort out your feelings is an important step because it puts a momentary halt to your automatic downward spiral into despair.

So, pause. Examine the emotions you are feeling right at that specific moment. Sometimes it helps to review a checklist in your mind.

- Am I angry?
- Am I frightened?
- Do I feel guilty?
- Do I feel hopeless?
- Do I feel rejected?
- Am I filled with dread?

You might discover you're angry because you feel rejected, and that scares you. Emotions can get so incredibly mixed together that it is often difficult to separate and pinpoint them exactly. Right now, you don't need to be exact. What you need at the moment is to STOP, focus on your emotions for a minute or two, and then acknowledge to yourself that you are experiencing unpleasant feelings.

Next question: *What am I thinking and saying to myself?* This question forces you to listen to and analyze your own irrational thinking and negative self-talk.

Remember, our feelings are not caused by outside circumstances, but by our perception and interpretation of those circumstances. If we're feeling a negative and distressing emotion, we're thinking a negative and distressing thought. We must listen to ourselves. Now is the time to acknowledge our automatic negative inner dialogue.

The next question to ask is: *What positive and rational self-statement can I make to challenge my depressive thoughts and feelings?*

Whenever you begin to feel depressed because you're engaging in negative and irrational thinking, you must examine your thinking and convince yourself in detail of the absurdity of your thoughts. Examine your irrational beliefs with a determination not to respect them or to let them dominate you. Whenever foolish and despairing thoughts burst into your consciousness, dissect them thoroughly and reject them as faulty. Don't punish yourself by stubbornly clinging to beliefs and notions that have no basis in fact.

As a summary, when you're getting depressed, STOP, and ask:

1. What am I feeling?
2. What am I thinking and saying to myself to trigger this feeling?
3. What positive and rational self-statements can I use to challenge my depressive thoughts and feelings?

The final step is to practice, practice, practice.

Now, we're going to look at some paper and pencil exercises we can use to retrain our minds to think in a more positive way.

Exercise 1: The Challenge List

Kay found herself sinking into a depressive fit when her fiance, Aaron, told her he was going to spend a holiday weekend with his parents in another city and he didn't invite her to come along. She felt hurt, sad, angry, and jealous — these feelings usually signaled a plunge into depression.

The next time you find yourself in a situation which causes negative feelings and you begin to spiral downward, STOP. Get a piece of paper and a pencil, and use them to challenge your depression.

1. List your emotions by writing: I feel _____ (deeply hurt, lonely, angry, scared).
2. Listen — *really listen* — to your negative, defeatist, irrational self-talk. On one half of the page, write down all the pessimistic, irrational, and self-punishing things you are saying to yourself. ("What a fool I've been!" "Nothing ever goes right for me." "I'll never have any happiness.")
3. Examine what you've written. Identify ideas that are overdemanding, unreasonable, unrealistic, nit-picking, negative, or mean-spirited.
4. Now, on the other half of the page, write down at least one positive challenge to each of your depressive thoughts. ("So I made a mistake. It's not the end of the world. Sure, I'm disappointed, but I'll live through it.")
5. Read over your list of positive challenges. Read them out loud. Concentrate on them. Commit them to your conscious mind in such a vivid and emphatic way that they will make an impression on your unconscious mind, which is the repository of all your negative beliefs. When you find yourself getting discouraged and making depressive self-statements, STOP! Take a deep breath. Now, draw on your repository of positive challenges.
6. Practice. Practice. Practice.

An excerpt from Kay's Challenge List:

NEGATIVE THOUGHTS	POSITIVE CHALLENGE
1. *Oh, God! Aaron's ashamed to have his parents meet me.*	1. Just because he's not taking me for this one trip doesn't mean he's ashamed of me. He introduced me to his sister and we got along fine.
2. *He probably has another girlfriend back home.*	2. That's silly. He has never given me any reason to believe he's interested in someone else and I've never caught him in a lie before, so why should I think he's lying now?
3. *How dare he go off without me!*	3. Why shouldn't he go off without me? I don't own him. I've visited my relatives before without taking him along. What's the big deal?
4. *I'll just die if he doesn't take me with him.*	4. Of course, I won't die! I may not like the idea a whole lot, but it's not the end of the world if I don't get my own way.
5. *If he really loved me, he wouldn't want to be away from me for even a few days.*	5. Occasionally I like to do things on my own without Aaron. Does that mean I don't love him? Of course not! I can stand some time away from him. The problem is that I want to be the one who decides when and where. There it is again! I always want to have my way.

Reviewing this exercise is not enough. It's important for us to actually practice it on our own thoughts and beliefs because it's easy for us to sit back and say, "Boy, that Kay really has some messed-up thinking." It's much more difficult for us to recognize our own irrational thinking patterns. We can't rid ourselves of our irrational beliefs until we recognize them. This exercise is an important step in helping us come to terms with the depressive thinking that exists behind our depressive feelings.

A Cognitive Challenge to Biochemistry

While the Challenge List is a cognitive exercise, it is a technique that can help us deal more effectively with unpleasant biochemical changes in our bodies. For example, many women suffer from premenstrual syndrome (PMS) during the week before menstruation begins. PMS is a physical disorder caused by the normal hormonal changes that occur during the monthly cycle. Many of PMS's symptoms, however, are emotional in nature. Feelings of irritation, moodiness, depression, and aggression are not uncommon. Some women find themselves constantly on the verge of tears, and those who are prone to depression sometimes find the week prior to their period especially difficult.

How a woman interprets the hormone-caused changes in her body and mood can have a direct effect on how well she copes with PMS. For example:

HARMFUL INTERPRETATION	HELPFUL INTERPRETATION
Oh, no. I feel awful. I can't stand it. I want to jump out of my skin. Am I going crazy? I don't understand what's happening to me. Why do the kids have to get on my nerves so much?	I feel bloated and jumpy again. I better check the calendar. This feels like PMS. I better cut down on salt and increase my B vitamins for the next week. This will be over in a few days. I can handle it. I'll make a point of trying to be extra patient with the kids because I might be more irritable than usual and it's not their fault.

Depressed or anxious people can also suffer from a variety of unpleasant physical sensations, including heart palpitations, choking sensations, dizziness, dry mouth, and tingling under the skin. If our heart beats a little fast after drinking five cups of coffee, we can put ourselves into a panic attack by exclaiming, "Oh, no! My heart! I'm dying!" Or we can say, "This is interesting. Every time I drink a lot of coffee I get palpitations. I guess I should cut down on caffeine. I better sit down for a minute until this passes."

If we have any doubts about our physical symptoms, it's wise to be checked out by our doctor. If our doctor tells us that we're basically sound but suffering from physical symptoms of an emotional problem, then try using the Challenge List whenever the symptoms occur. If we change our cognitions, it's possible to alleviate the severity of biochemically-caused physical and emotional symptoms. Try it! It really does work.

A note: At first, writing down our thoughts and challenges can seem cumbersome and time-consuming. But we must remember that this new process is a skill, and it takes time to learn. After sufficient practice, positive thinking can become almost as automatic as negative thinking. Until then, it is vital to practice, practice, practice this new skill with paper and pencil.

Now, let's look at another method of challenging our depressive beliefs.

Family Rules

It would seem that we would know our own rules and expectations. Surprisingly, few of us do. We don't take the time to analyze the basis of our beliefs or to question whether or not the values we live by are helpful or harmful to us.

For most of us, the main source of our beliefs is the value system we learned as children from the words and deeds of our parents. As one depressed friend named Dennis told us, "I learned chronic dissatisfaction at my daddy's knee. I can remember when I was little — it was even before I started kindergarten — on Sunday nights at home there would be this tense feeling about Monday coming. My dad would grumble about the grind of being a wage slave and how much he hated his job. And as it got darker and darker outside, the gloom inside grew just as black. Ever since I can remember, I dreaded Monday and hated school and my jobs. No matter how satisfying my work was, I always felt as if liking my job would be a sign of disloyalty to my old man."

As we enter adolescence and young adulthood, we incorporate some of the values of the outside world into our belief system — lessons from friends, church, school, and the media. Unfortunately, a very large part of the teachings we receive from our families and from the outside world may have no rational foundation at all. Yet, as children, we have no way of knowing this. Like Dennis, we simply believe that the lessons we're given are wise, just, and right. We accept them as they're presented, internalizing them and making them an unquestioned part of our belief system. Gradually, as we grow older, we forget where these values came from and the punishments we received as children for violating them. All we know is that we feel vaguely awful whenever we do anything which violates these deeply held conscious and unconscious beliefs, for we know intuitively that a violation of these rules always brings punishment.

Depression is one of the punishments we inflict on ourselves when we don't live up to our internalized laws.

The following exercise gives an opportunity to examine some of the values we learned as children.

Exercise 2: Ten Commandments Exercise
Step One

Take out a pencil and a few sheets of paper. At the top of the first sheet write: "THE TEN FAMILY COMMANDMENTS I LEARNED FROM MY PARENTS." Ask: *What Ten Commandments best summarize the expectations and beliefs my family advocated for me either through verbal lessons or by example?* List them.

This is what Kay's list looked like:

1. My job is to make my mother happy.
2. Daddy loves a daughter who is sweet and pretty.
3. Don't embarrass the family.
4. Into every life a little rain must fall.
5. To be happy a man needs money, and a woman needs good looks so she can get a man with money.
6. Girls should be cute and shouldn't act too smart; if I act sweet and nice and helpless, I can get someone to take care of me.
7. I should never make mistakes; if I do, I should feel terrible about it.
8. I'm supposed to excel in everything I do or else the people who love me will be embarrassed by me.
9. Protect yourself from outside criticism. Sometimes I just want to roll up in a ball. I'm chronically defensive.
10. I shouldn't put myself first. I should be happy to take care of other people; if I do things right, they'll appreciate me and make me happy in return.

Step Two

After making the list, examine it closely. Do the rules you live by benefit you? Or do they set the stage for depressive thoughts and gloomy moods? When Kay looked at her own set of Ten Commandments, she decided that nine of the ten rules she lived by were irrational and contributed to her unhappiness. (She thought the fourth rule was rational because it helped her keep her life in perspective.)

Kay wanted to change her rules because they caused an unconscious pattern of thoughts, feelings, and behavior which made her feel unhappy, inferior, and worthless. In order to live up to her old rules she would have to be: (a) responsible for the happiness of others (impossible to do because each of us can be responsible only for our own feelings); (b) a perfect person who never makes mistakes (also impossible to do because everyone makes mistakes and no one is perfect); (c) always sweet, always pretty, always slim, and submissive, and not too smart in order to be loved (an insulting suggestion to any woman born in the twentieth century); (d) ashamed, mortified, and depressed whenever she didn't meet conditions a, b, and c (who needs it!).

Before Kay practiced these exercises, she was only dimly aware of the rules by which she lived. "I had never really stopped to think about it before," she told us. "I just accepted that I was supposed to look and act a certain way, and if I didn't, I was a worthless, hopeless, unlovable creature. I didn't know I had other options."

Now, pause for a moment. What about you? Have you explored other options? Or are you still trying to measure up to an unrealistic belief system of which you are only dimly aware? Could your misery, guilt, and depression be the result of constantly failing to live up to impossible standards?

If our conscience is well-developed, we feel guilty, frightened, or ashamed when we violate the rules of our moral upbringing. Besides cultural admonitions against violence, lying, stealing, killing, and sexual abuse, there are family rules such as: "Don't ever upset your mother." "Don't embarrass the family." "Always make a good impression."

Now, here comes the tricky part. Our irrational and unreasonable unconscious minds demand that we live up to each and every one of these laws. The rule, "Don't upset Mother" can carry as much emotional weight as, "Don't murder innocent women and children."

In order to break through depression and avoid feelings of shame, guilt, fear, anger, and hopelessness, we must behave in a way that is consistent with our conscience. To do this, we must either conform to all the irrational and infantile beliefs in our conscious and unconscious minds, or we can change the rules that harm us.

Exercise 3: Changing the Rules

Step One

Pick one of the irrational rules you'd like to change. Now, using pencil and paper, describe how this rule affects you. How does it cause you trouble? How does it make you feel? And remember, this isn't a make-work assignment to get a grade in English Comp. Don't worry about grammar, punctuation, or spelling. Let your thoughts and feelings flow, or tumble, naturally.

The following is from Kay's list:

I always think it's my job to make my mother happy. She's extremely unhappy with her life. My dad drinks too much and there's always enough money for what he wants, but never enough for the things my mother wants and needs. Things are unpleasant at home and I avoid going over there even though I love both my parents very much. I feel guilty because I should be doing something to make my mother happy, but it is too depressing to hear her complaining all the time. I try to give her advice about how to handle Dad and about getting a job so she can afford things on her own, but she never listens. She wants a grandchild and I haven't given her one and that makes me feel like I'm a bad daughter. I always dread her questions about when I'm going to get married because I know I've let her down again. It's like if I were more attractive, I'd be married and have kids and then my mother would be happy, so my being overweight is a direct insult to her happiness. I want my mother to be happy and I feel just terrible because I can't solve her problems and make her feel better. I worry about this all the time. Whenever I do something — change my hair, make a mistake, get an award, have sex, stay out late — I always worry about "what will Mother think about this?" I always seem to have the burden of my mother's opinion hanging over me. If something bad happens, worry about my mother's reaction always makes it worse. And if something good happens I want to run right over and tell her because I think it will make her happy; but it never does, so I can't enjoy my successes either.

Step Two

List all of the ways in which this rule is unreasonable and destructive.

Here's what Kay listed:

This rule is irrational, unreasonable, and destructive to me because:

1. In reality, my successes and failures belong to me, not to my mother.
2. I love my mother, but I can't live her life for her.
3. Why should I suffer because my mother doesn't want to change? What she does with her life is her choice, not mine.
4. This rule is based on the idea that I have some kind of power to give or to take away happiness from other people.
5. Getting married and having a baby in order to satisfy my mother is unfair to me and plain silly!
6. If my mother is unhappy because of my weight, that's her problem and not mine. I don't love her any more or less depending on what she weighs. What makes me think she loves me less because I'm heavy?
7. I realize both my parents have personal problems and I want to be helpful and supportive, but I am not a therapist or a doctor; I have neither the expertise nor the knowledge needed to solve their problems.
8. I'm trying to do something that is not within my power, so I always fail at achieving my goal, and failure makes me feel bad.

9. Maybe if I truly love my mother, I'll accept her the way she is and stop trying to change her.

10. I accept the fact that at times I have done things to my mother that made us both feel bad — like lying to her, yelling at her, breaking her best vase, and driving her car without permission. I am willing to take responsibility for my misconduct. But it is not my fault if my mother doesn't get along with my dad, if she doesn't like her house, if she feels bad about how many wrinkles she's getting, or if she feels shy and nervous in a crowd. I can be sympathetic and understanding toward her, but it is not my responsibility to solve her problems.

Step Three

If you've convinced yourself the rule is unreasonable and destructive, you can change it. Think up a new rule for your life. While you're thinking, be sure to ask:

• Is the new rule realistic?
• Is it attainable?
• Is it likely not to be harmful to me or anyone else?

Consider various possibilities until you come up with a rule you value and respect. Write the new rule on paper. Read it several times. Try it on for size. Is it reasonable? Healthy? Is it accepting of human limitations? Will it enhance your life? Is it a rule you'd be proud to share with your children?

If you can answer "yes" to all those questions, you've probably come up with a pretty good rule.

This is how Kay framed her new rule: "It is not my job to solve all my mother's problems."

Step Four

Framing a new rule doesn't mean we'll live by it. The old rule is deeply embedded in our unconscious minds, and we must superimpose our new rule over it.

Write down your new rule on an index card or a piece of paper. Read it out loud three times. Memorize it. For the next ten days, remember to repeat your new rule out loud to yourself three times daily. Say it gently, without anger, perhaps as you're looking in the mirror as you wash up in the morning, or as you drive to work, or when you're ready for bed. Whenever you find yourself falling under the spell of the old, negative rule, silently repeat the new rule to yourself a few times. But don't overdo it! Your mind will accept the new rule if you repeat it gently, calmly, and lovingly. Let it slide into your unconscious mind; don't try to force it in there.

Step Five

Changing an old, destructive rule into a new, positive one takes courage, thought, and study. Most of all, it takes ACTION.

Let's begin a third list. What actions are you going to take so you can start living by your new, life-enhancing rule? Write down the positive steps you're willing to take.

This is from Kay's list:

1. I'll practice positive self-talk. I'll repeat the new rule to myself every day and tell myself why it's a good change.
2. I'll behave in an uncritical and kind fashion toward my mother, and I won't tell her what she should do to be happy.
3. I'll educate myself about family alcohol problems, and I'll make this material available to my mother; but I won't demand that she use it.
4. When my mother starts complaining about how bad her life is, I'll express sympathy and I'll suggest she see a professional counselor because I don't know how to solve her problems for her.
5. I won't expect things to change overnight.
6. If I can't work this problem out by myself, I'll find a professional counselor to help me.

Keep the lists and review them on a regular basis. As you become comfortable with a change, you can move on to another one. The process of creating new rules is not a one-shot deal. The real danger is to think the old rules can never be altered. With practice, you'll be able to identify and change more and more of your old destructive beliefs.

Although your new rules may not be well-formulated yet, they are a start on building a happier, new life. In time, you may want to refine and change your new rules. And you can!

Summary of Changing the Rules Exercise

Step 1. Identify a rule or message you would like to change.

Step 2. List the ways in which this rule is unreasonable or harmful to you.

Step 3. Frame a new rule that is reasonable and beneficial.

Step 4. Commit your new rule to memory and practice embedding it in your unconscious mind.

Step 5. List the actions you must take to put this new rule into effect.

Step 6. Review your progress regularly.

Chapter Nine

Self-Care:
The Foundation of Recovery

Part I: Small Deeds

"Better do to no end, than nothing," counseled Robert Burton in *The Anatomy of Melancholy*. Burton, a seventeenth century scholar, wrote this remarkable book as an exercise in self-help to combat his own depression. Over 350 years later, Burton's advice to the depressed remains valid.

Writer Percy Knauth repeats the advice in a memoir of his own depression. The only way to break the cycle of brooding thoughts, says Knauth, in *A Season in Hell*, is to act.

"Act?" asks the depressed person whose motivation to do anything at all is worm-belly low. "How?"

Says Knauth, "Do something, anything. It really doesn't matter what, as long as it is a positive action." In the season he spent in a personal hell of depression, Knauth forced himself to do three simple things.

1. He got out of bed.
2. He made himself some coffee.
3. He made the bed.

Do these small acts seem too trivial to mention? Such small acts are definitely not trivial if you're immobilized by depression, as Knauth was. Getting back to the rock-bottom basics by doing something — *anything* — can be the foundation of recovery from depression.

What did Knauth's three small deeds demonstrate?

It proved to me, day after day, that I was still able to accomplish *something*, even though my mind was telling me I was a total loss. By the act of getting out of bed I proved that I could still command my body and had a semblance of free will. By the act of making coffee, I proved that I could still do something to preserve myself and thus deny my growing wish for death. By the act of making my bed I proved that I had not fallen completely into the state of sloth and disarray that my disorganized mind constantly told me I was in; I still cared.

These small beginnings led to larger accomplishments— what Knauth calls "the primitive foundations on which later, with the help of [medication] and psychotherapy, I could rebuild my self-esteem."

What's the Use?

When we're depressed we often want to withdraw from all activity. We want to stay in bed. We want to blot out worries, cares, and obligations. It's like, in the song by the rock group, The Eagles, we've checked into Hotel California, where "you can check out anytime you want, but you can never leave."

The central problem all depressed people face is the feeling that we're powerless to do anything to relieve our depression. We're caught in a web of hopelessness, and our struggle to go on seems as futile as the fluttering of a moth caught firmly in the snares of a spiderweb.

The important questions we must ask ourselves are these:

Am I doing everything I can to mobilize my resources to fight off this depression?

Or . . .

Have I yielded, given up, abandoned the struggle?

The depressed person wants to scream, "Of course, I'm doing everything in my power to overcome my depression! Do you think I like being this way? Do you think I ENJOY being depressed?"

Dejected and pessimistic, we say to ourselves, "There's nothing I can do. Nothing." And we stare into space, only vaguely aware of the flickering light reflected from the strangely meaningless images on TV. Overwhelmed by a pervasive sense of futility, we think, what's the use . . . what's the point of doing anything at all?

The point is this: We cannot solve all our problems, present and future, at once. We cannot put all our worries and cares to rest and find instant happiness.

But we can take small steps that will help us in our fight against depression. These small steps aren't glamorous cure-alls. They are the essentials of self-care and other small deeds that pave the way for recovery.

What to Do When You Can't Do Anything

1. *Eat.* Depressed people sometimes act as if they believe chocolate is an essential vitamin. It's not. Try to eat a varied diet. Get the basic protein, vitamins, and minerals needed to fuel the body and the brain. We tend to get so involved and preoccupied in thought that we overlook the fact that our thoughts are generated by brain cells that need nourishment. At a minimum, we must eat at least one good, balanced meal a day.

2. *Move.* Physical activity can be an extremely important factor in recovery from depression. Exercise keeps our muscles toned up and gets oxygen into those dark and musty crevasses in the brain. Exercise doesn't have to take the form of a marathon or a Jane Fonda workout. Walk. Walk upstairs instead of using the elevator. Walk to the store. Take a walk in the park. Walk to church. But try to walk at least ten minutes every day.

3. *Wash.* Take a shower or a bath daily to keep the depression cooties from taking over your body. Brush your teeth. Comb your hair. Shave or put on makeup. Wear clean clothes. These simple grooming rituals can be a

vitally important ingredient in retaining your dignity and self-esteem.

4. *Chop wood.* Or do anything else that will get you outdoors. Staying in bed in a dark room lit only by a 40-watt lamp and the flickering TV is not — repeat *not* — conducive to recovery from depression. Research shows that some depressed people (no one knows how many) suffer from "seasonal affective disorder," which means that their depression is linked to the amount of sunlight they receive. Naturally, they get most depressed in winter, when the days are shorter. One of the ways to deal with this kind of depression is to spend more time outdoors, away from artificial lighting. It may also help to get full-spectrum light bulbs at home (such as Vita Lights, which are available in most large variety and hardware stores). And don't forget the important psychological boost that can come from simply pulling open the curtains and letting the sunshine in.

Self-Motivation

The four suggestions previously mentioned are the building blocks of recovery from depression. These are the things we can do when we can't do anything else. Of course, motivation is very important here, and we must face the issue squarely. We must ask ourselves the question: "Am I really doing everything I can do to overcome my depression?"

If it's been a week since our last bath or shower, then we must answer, "No."

If we subsist on red wine and soda crackers, or if our main dish for three or four days in a row is a cold macaroni casserole, then we must answer, "No."

If we spend long hours in a darkened room huddled up under bedding that hasn't been washed for a while, then we must answer, "No."

In short, when we're "too depressed to do anything" we probably haven't thought about taking care of the small things we have grown careless about. Self-care is essential to recovery from depression. Robert Burton's instructions on the small deeds that help lift us from depression remain sound: "Better do to no end, than nothing."

One important area of self-care deserves special mention: the controversial role of alcohol and other drugs in causing and maintaining depression.

Part II: Chemical In-dependency

"The problems of alcoholism and drug abuse have strong links to depression," observes Dr. Nathan Kline. "The search for highs may often begin as a flight from lows."

It's true that the chronically depressed person often appears to use alcohol or other mood-changing drugs as a form of solace, as a kind of self-medication providing momentary relief from confusion and woe. Alcohol and other drugs may also ease self-doubt by soaking the psyche in a bath of chemical confidence. So, indeed, the flight from lows can culminate in the search for chemical highs — or as Shakespeare wrote, "some sweet oblivious antidote" to cares and troubles.

But it's just as true that psychiatrists and other therapists sometimes treat depressed people for years without recognizing that the depression is frequently tied to chemical dependency. Depression has traditionally been a more acceptable diagnosis than alcoholism, and many alcoholics have been admitted repeatedly to hospitals for "exhaustion" or "depression" when, in fact, they are suffering from chemical dependency.

It is one of the triumphs of the alcoholism treatment movement that alcoholism is now widely considered to be a primary disorder — rather than a symptom of some underlying depression — and that most states require insurance companies to cover treatment for chemical dependency.

Nevertheless, some chemically dependent people are still reluctant to admit they have problems with alcohol or other drugs. This is especially true if we're also depressed. We don't want our depressive moods ignored, and we certainly don't want to be told we're only making our depression worse by continuing to use alcohol or other drugs. We may not want to hear that we would be less depressed if we took better care of ourselves. If we were to admit alcohol or other drugs play an important role in keeping us depressed, miserable, and unhappy, then our continued use of chemicals begins to look as if we actually want to remain depressed.

Of course, we don't want to remain miserable. But we also don't want our deeply felt despondency to be diagnosed as a result of our personal habits. That's like telling someone who experiences mystical peak experiences that her attunement with the Universal Force is due to an overdose of chocolate. What an insult! Paradoxically, if we're feeling crushed under the weight of the world, it actually helps our shaky self-esteem if we imagine our problems as deep, intricate, and inscrutable mysteries beyond our control, rather than self-imposed troubles that can be alleviated by something as simple as living alcohol- and drug-free.

Use vs. Abuse

At this point we want to stress that we're not talking only about chronic alcoholism or chronic addiction to prescription medication or so-called "recreational drugs." We are talking about the use — often the careless use — of alcohol, cocaine, marijuana, prescription downers, and other drugs. The links between depression and the use of alcohol or other drugs cover more territory than just the alcoholism-addiction-depression connection. We must take into consideration alcohol and other drug *use* — not abuse or addiction only.

The attempt to quiet distressing emotions by alcohol use always backfires in the long run. Alcohol is a depressant drug. While drinking may momentarily blot out pain, the fact remains that even small amounts of alcohol can cause depression or intensify existing bad feelings in vulnerable people.

It has often been noted that depressed people suffer from feelings of guilt and inadequacy. When alcohol is a factor in one's depression, the guilt and inadequacy are often based on reality. Drinking may set the stage for a relaxation of social controls and give a person "time out" from the ordinary responsibilities of life. The guilt comes from behaving badly, from violating social taboos, and from violating one's own personal integrity and higher values.

In recent years, the cocaine-depression cycle has come to the attention of clinicians and researchers. Cocaine produces short, powerful highs, followed by "crashes" — periods of agitation and depression. Richard Smart described this pattern in his book, *The Snow Papers*, a "memoir of illusion" about his years of casual cocaine use and eventual addiction.

"It was common knowledge," writes Smart, "that a lot of heavy coke users often suffered deep, crippling depressions when they came down from the drug, but I had never been one of them." He avoided the depressions for years by being "hot-wired on coke and mellowed on champagne." But there came a time when he was no longer able to mellow out.

I felt a kind of depression even when I was *on* the drug, which was nearly all the time. Not a crippling depression . . . a shadow of disquiet and despair that constantly lurked below the surface of my energy and restless movement.

When cocaine users slide into regular use and addiction, they frequently begin to use alcohol more intensely to smooth out the agitation and depression that inevitably comes when there are no more drugs. So it was with Smart.

I needed coke in the morning before breakfast and all day and all evening long. And to keep the wired edginess in check, I needed alcohol all day and all evening with it. There weren't many emotional ups and downs in those last hazy months, because I was wired and semi-

103

drunk all the time. I moved about on a flat plain, accompanied everywhere by futility.

Thus, alcoholism can become an unforeseen side effect of coke addiction.

Three Rules of Abstinence

With these facts in mind, there are three rules or guidelines to follow regarding the use of alcohol and other mood-altering chemicals by depressed people or by people who have a family history of depression.

Rule 1. Depression cannot be reliably relieved if the depressed person continues using alcohol or other drugs. In other words, we cannot have our pot or our booze and expect to get lasting — or even temporary — relief from depression. An important fact to remember is that alcohol and other drugs interact with antidepressant medications, and people taking antidepressants should always avoid the use of alcohol and other drugs — under any circumstances.

Rule 2. Do not attempt to cure alcoholism or other forms of chemical dependency by dealing with the "underlying depression." Chemical dependency is a primary disease and must be dealt with directly, not as a symptom of depression. Most experts agree on one thing: *The only reliable recovery from chemical dependency is firmly based on abstinence from alcohol or other drugs.* If a person is both chemically dependent and depressed, the chemical dependency must be dealt with first. This is because it's impossible to adequately diagnose and treat depression in a person who is still actively drinking or abusing other drugs.

Far too many alcoholics have spent thousands of dollars and have wasted years in psychoanalysis or other forms of therapy trying to overcome an addiction by resolving the "underlying depression." Unfortunately, there is no consumer protection agency for troubles of the mind. This approach to treatment, however, is becoming increasingly obsolete.

One point of vital importance for all depressed people to understand is this: The tendency to develop chemical dependency problems is often an inherited, biological characteristic. There's also a growing body of research pointing to heredity as a major factor in depression. While alcoholism and depression are two separate and distinct disorders, there is reason to believe they may be biologically linked. In other words, while chemical dependency and depression are different disorders, they often go hand in hand. This line of reasoning points to an obvious conclusion: Depression can be triggered or augmented by the use of alcohol or other drugs on a regular basis.

This conclusion suggests another rule.

Rule 3. To prevent depression or to reduce the intensity of future episodes of depression, avoid the use of alcohol and other so-called "recreational drugs," including marijuana, cocaine, and tobacco products.

Most people don't understand this simple but important fact: we don't have to be an alcoholic to have a problem with alcohol; we don't have to be an addict or a mainliner or a coke fiend to have a problem with other drugs.

If our life is a mess, and if we drink or smoke dope or take prescription pills in order to help ourselves get through the bad times, then we have a problem. Drinking and doing other drugs is not a healthy way to cope with the miseries of life.

We want to get a bit dogmatic here and say that a person can't become reliably free from depression for any length of time unless he or she is free from the use of drugs. Antidepressant medication is the one important exception to this rule. Anti-depressants are neither intoxicating nor addictive. They don't make you high and they don't get you hooked.

What about tobacco? The relationship between smoking

and chronic bad feelings should be obvious. If you have a life-style that degrades your body, small wonder you feel below par much of the time.

We should ask ourselves honestly, "Do drugs really add anything positive to my life? Do they really make things better, or is that just an illusion? Do I really need drugs in my life?"

If we do decide to become drug-free, we may find it's harder than we thought. We can get help if we need it. We don't have to check into a hospital for a month. Many major treatment centers now provide outpatient counseling. Or call Alcoholics Anonymous, Narcotics Anonymous, Pot Smokers Anonymous, or the Cocaine Hotline.

Whatever step you take, take it with the positive thought in mind that you're not giving up something of value. You are taking a vital step toward self-care that can only add to the quality of your life. You don't have to allow chemical dependency to fuel your depression, distort your thoughts, and rule your moods.

Chapter Ten

Chronic Low-Grade Depression

For many years, neurologists have studied the fascinating phenomenon of the "phantom" limb. When a person loses an arm or leg or finger to amputation, he or she will almost always retain the sense that the limb is still there. We're not talking about wishful thinking or anything like that; the leg is gone, and the amputee knows it. But the nerves that run from the stump of the amputated limb to the spinal cord and brain tell the amputee that the leg is still there.

Some phantom limbs are sensed as being ghost-like and unreal, while others are perceived as vividly lifelike. One man who lost his right leg just above the knee suffered excruciating pain every day. He visited his physician and said, "I think I'm going crazy, Doc. I can't stand the pain."

The doctor examined the man's stump. "Does it hurt here?" he asked, touching the man's thigh.

"No, Doc," the man said. "It's down lower. On my ankle, right where my foot used to connect to my leg."

The patient wasn't crazy. The phantom limb phenomenon is caused by real neurological impulses which fool the brain into thinking that the missing limb is still there. The phantom sensation can be useful. The amputee can use the ghost neurological impulses to help control and incorporate an artificial limb into his or her body image, thus enabling an amputee to walk and move as if the artificial leg is a part of the body. If the phantom sensations are strong enough, the amputee will feel as if a real flesh and blood foot is hitting the ground.

Dr. Oliver Sacks tells of a man whose phantom limb disappeared when he slept. Every morning the man had to "wake up" his phantom. Dr. Sacks describes the ritual this way: "First he flexes the thigh-stump towards him, and then he slaps it sharply — like a baby's bottom — several times." On the fifth or sixth slap the phantom suddenly shoots forth, rekindled, reanimated by the stimulation. "Only then can he put on his prosthesis and walk."

Now, what does this have to do with depression?

Slapping Depression Awake Every Morning

By the time Tom landed his first job as an assistant professor of psychology at a small college, he had almost given up hope of realizing his dreams of academic success. But here he was at age 40, with his Ph.D. in one hand and a teaching contract in the other; finally, after years of struggle, scrimping, deprivation, and doubt, he was on the verge of making his dream come true.

Life as a divorced middle-aged graduate student had been tough and lonely. Tom had come up the hard way, without family assistance, without a woman who loved him. He had to work a series of degrading, low-paying, part-time jobs to stay in school, and he had been forced to live in dark, squalid little apartments to make his meager paychecks stretch far enough to meet school expenses.

Tom had won several awards and honors and was the top grad student in the psychology department, but when he compared himself to the other students he felt he didn't measure up. "They were just kids," he said. "Bright kids — 22 or 23 years old, with affluent parents who were footing the bills for their bright, shiny children."

Tom was almost twenty years older than most of his classmates, not so shiny, and if he hadn't been able to write better papers or speak more authoritatively than a kid living on Daddy's expense account, then there was something seriously wrong in the universe. So, even taking the awards into consideration, Tom's years as a grad student had been hell.

But all that was changing now. He had a good job, exactly the kind he'd been working toward, with excellent pay; and, miracle of miracles, he'd found a woman, Allie, who loved him. Maybe it was true, maybe life did begin at 40.

Tom and Allie moved into a big house only a few blocks from campus. No more dark rat holes, but a real house. Tom had spent nearly twenty years working and slaving and dreaming about the kind of life he wanted to live, and now his plans were coming true. He had everything he thought he'd need to be happy — a good job, great pay, status and respect in the community, a loving woman, a neat house, and enough money to buy clothes, a car, and a few luxuries.

So, if Tom had finally acquired the external trappings of happiness, why was he still so miserable? Why, when the alarm clock rang in the morning, did he roll over muttering, "Oh, God, another day already. I can't stand it. How long are people supposed to live like this? I wish one morning I just wouldn't wake up."

Have you ever experienced a situation like Tom's? Have you struggled to meet a goal, thinking you'd find happiness at the end of that rainbow, and once you got there you found yourself just as empty and sad as before? Our unhappiness often baffles our friends and family. "Look," they chide us. "You have exactly what you wanted. You should be happy. What's your problem?"

We have known people — clients, friends, and relatives — who have struggled through difficult and depressing situations where the only thing that kept them going was a golden dream of the future. And many of them did make their dreams come true — they graduated from law school, or bought the house, or had the baby, or got the promotion or man or woman or job they wanted. Some of these people found happiness at the end of their personal rainbow, others found only fool's gold. No matter what our unhappy friends attain, achieve, or accomplish, it is never enough to bring on anything more than fleeting moments of satisfaction. Why do they remain so unhappy and depressed when they are surrounded by love, comfort, and success? Why can't they enjoy what they have worked so hard to attain?

We think it is because, in many ways, they are like amputees suffering from phantom pain. Many of us wake up in the morning and slap our depressions awake with a barrage of negative self-talk. After the fifth or sixth slap, our depression shoots forth, rekindled and reanimated by the stimulation. Only then do we feel normal — because, you see, to us misery is normal. If we were to face the day in a good mood, with hope and high expectations, we wouldn't know how to act.

Depression as Self-Defense

While our depressive symptoms may cause us much misery and pain, they also have some beneficial side effects.

1. Depression can excuse us — in our own eyes and in the eyes of others — from having to be fully functioning, responsible people who are accountable for our own successes and failures.
2. We can use our symptoms to evoke sympathy and reassurance from those around us.
3. By focusing on our inadequacies and weaknesses, we can lower other people's expectations of us, thus relieving the pressure to perform and achieve.
4. We can induce others to protect and take care of us.
5. We can have an excuse for taking "time out" from stressful or threatening situations.
6. We can use our depression as an excuse for failure and as a defense against self-criticism and criticism from others.

Tom, the 40-year-old beginning college professor, discovered he was using his depression as a defense against his fear of failure. His new job scared him stiff. What if his students didn't like him? What if the other faculty members thought his academic preparation was shallow? What if his department head found him stupid and boring and unintellectual? If any of these fears came true, Tom was sunk. The college wouldn't renew his contract, and Tom would have to explain to his family and friends and his professors back at his alma mater why he hadn't lived up to their expectations. How humiliating! In order to save face, he'd have to have a pretty damn good explanation for his failure.

And so, without being consciously aware of what he was doing, Tom started creating an excuse strategy for failure, with depression as his main defensive weapon.

Later, Tom confided, "I kept telling myself, 'The reason you're not performing up to standard is because you've got this terrible case of depression.' I'd have these fantasies where I was in a courtroom where my older brother was the judge and the jury was made up of my other relatives and their friends and some of my teachers. And when they demanded an explanation for why I was such a miserable screw-up, I'd plead not guilty by reason of insanity. Then I'd parade out all my depressive symptoms as witnesses in my behalf. 'See,' I'd tell them. 'I could have succeeded except I had all these problems to contend with. So, don't be so hard on me.' In this scenario, I was a victim of circumstances beyond my control and everyone was supposed to understand and feel sorry for me."

The big problem was that by slapping his depression awake every morning so he could have a phantom to blame his potential failure on, Tom was creating a situation that almost guaranteed he would fail.

Let's think about our own situation.

- Do you feel under tremendous pressure to succeed at whatever you do?
- Do you believe you must excel in your job and personal

relationships?
- Do you fear rejection and failure?
- Does the thought of disappointing the people you care about fill you with shame?
- Do you sometimes think you can't stand one more humiliation?

No one likes to fail. No one. And it doesn't matter whether you're a big and important person or otherwise. Maybe you're worried about negotiating a million dollar deal. Or maybe you're trying to win the love and respect of your stepchildren. Or you want to run a household smoothly. Or win a bowling tournament. It doesn't matter exactly what it is you're worried about. If the fear of failure looms large in your mind, it is only natural for you to construct a defense against this threat to your self-esteem.

Depressive symptoms may have real value to us if they offer protection from what seems like the pain of public shame and condemnation for failure. We may secretly cling to our misery so when the time comes we can plead, "Not guilty, your honor. You see, I screwed up because I wasn't well. That wasn't really me who failed, it was my depression that caused all the problems. But me — the real me — well, I'm innocent. And I feel just terrible about everything. So, you see, your honor, I don't deserve to be punished." Unfortunately, chronic low-grade depression is not really a convincing self-defense against failure. We use it as an excuse, a cop-out, and we're afraid others might discover our deception. Rightfully so, for in time they will see that our depressions flower conveniently whenever we get under stress.

Instead of expending all that energy defending against failure, we need to find better ways to increase the likelihood of success. Whether it be in school or a job or in a personal relationship, we must create a mental attitude that will allow us to succeed.

To do this, we must root out the negative, failure statements that constantly run through our consciousness and replace them with positive, success statements that are so vivid and emphatic that they penetrate through our layers of fear and doubt right down into our subconscious mind. If habitual negativity is part of our mind-set, our conscious, intellectual mind can be a great barrier to happiness. While it's important to use our powers of rational thought to over-come chronic low-grade depression, it's also important to make use of the wonderful, almost mystical, powers of our subconscious mind.

Tom's older brother, Trask, is a prime example of an intelli-gent, educated person who made himself chronically misera-ble by being ultrasmart, analytical, and intellectually alert. Let's take a look at how he used the considerable powers of his intellect to stay depressed. Then, let's examine a specific technique that can be used to break through intellectual nega-tivity in order to tap into the healing powers of the subcon-scious mind.

Habitual Negativity: The Power of Negative Thinking

Trask knew that a dark cloud lurked behind every silver lining. If you showed him a glass half full of water, Trask would see a glass half empty. And then he'd comment on the hazards of fluoridation, water pollution, acid rain, and the vanishing water tables of Phoenix, Arizona and the San Joaquin Valley in California.

Things like that stuck in his mind. His personal motto came from a joke printed on a sign in a mechanic's shop. The sign went like this:

They said it couldn't be done
So I tackled it with a grin,
. . . and I couldn't do it either.

"Always expect the worst," said Trask. "That way you'll never be disappointed." When he was eight years old, Trask received his first and most lasting major disappointment. In a blinding flash of insight, he came face-to-face with the awe-some infinitude of the universe and discovered his own mortality. Perhaps it is no coincidence that Trask had been an only child until he was eight years old. So at nine he was a has-been, jilted both by the universe and by his doting parents.

As he grew older, Trask seemed to gravitate naturally toward the futility of existence. He felt a shock of recognition when he first heard Simon and Garfunkel sing, "Hello darkness my old friend, Come to visit me again . . . " And he learned by heart the melancholy soliloquy of Shakespeare's *Macbeth*:

Tomorrow, and tomorrow, and tomorrow
Creeps in this petty pace from day to day,
To the last syllable of recorded time;
And all our yesterdays have lighted fools
The way to dusty death. Out, out, brief candle!
Life's but a walking shadow, a poor player
That struts and frets his hour upon the stage
And then is heard no more. It is a tale
Told by an idiot, full of sound and fury,
Signifying nothing.

Strong stuff, old Shakespeare, telling it like it is. Of course, Trask was always disappointed because he was really a secret idealist, and a very frustrated one, as most secret idealists are. In *People in Quandaries*, Wendall Johnson pointed out that people like Trask are suffering from the IFD syndrome: they *Idealize* situations and people; they invariably get *Frustrated*; and their sense of futility leads to *Depression*.

Trask's whole existence was one chronic low-grade depression. He had few friends because few people could bear his gloomy outlook on the world. When his sister, Joyce, had her first baby, Trask ignored the blessed event. When she had her second baby a few years later, Trask sent her a copy of Paul Ehrlich's scathing indictment of overpopulation, *The Population Bomb*.

Strangely enough, Trask's wife, Annette, loved her husband despite his doom-mongering, his cynical contempt, and his dour and gloomy disposition. She was good at pepping herself up with positive thoughts, and she finally convinced Trask that he might feel better about himself and the world if he tried to eliminate his negative thinking and focus on positive thinking.

"Where do I start?" Trask asked, then said, "I feel tired already. I mean this is a monumental task."

"Well, you could start by reading some of Norman Vincent Peale," Annette suggested. "Or by listening to some of his tapes. I have some tapes you could use."

"Norman Vincent Peale," Trask said, and the disgust dripped from his voice as if he'd bitten into a piece of toast covered with shower curtain mildew.

"Have you ever really read Norman Vincent Peale or listened to what he has to say?"

"Well, no . . . but . . ."

"So why don't you find out for yourself?"

Why not, indeed? Trask asked himself. After a little more urging, Trask decided to humor her. After all, it might not hurt to spend an hour or two with the great Positive Thinker.

Surprisingly, Trask was impressed when he listened to one of Peale's inspirational tapes on positive images. Peale was a pretty straightforward and convincing speaker. "Select one of those problems that loom so large in your mind and take action against it," counseled Peale. He even quoted Ralph Waldo Emerson: "Do the thing you fear, and the death of fear is certain."

Well, yes, Trask thought, it sounds good.

Then Peale related how important it is to believe in yourself and "to get a deep sense of the presence of God in your life." Peale went on to say, "Imagine yourself walking alongside the power that created the tiniest flower and holds the constellations in their places. That is the surest way to cast out all fears and shrinking and sense of failure."

Trask stopped the tape and pondered the suggestion. Try as he might, Trask could get no satisfaction from thinking about the tiniest flower, nor was he inspired by ruminating on the laws of physics, particularly the second law of thermodynamics — or entropy — which states that eventually everything runs down.

Still, Trask continued to listen. With great eloquence, Peale advised praying, going to church, and reading the Bible. He related the well-known story of David and Goliath. David's sling and stones were the smallest part of his armament in his clash with the giant Goliath. "Thou comest to me with a sword and with a spear and a shield," David taunted Goliath. "But I come to thee in the name of the Lord of Hosts."

"In other words," Peale commented with approval, "David went to battle supported by a God-saturated mind. That was his powerful armament. Therefore, he knew no fear, and therefore he was victorious."

Trask stopped the tape again. Whoa, he thought. The powerful armament of a God-saturated mind has fueled every form of religious fanaticism and persecution. Trask also wondered how many rounds David would have lasted with Goliath if he'd met the giant at Caesar's Palace in Las Vegas with sixteen ounce gloves instead of a slingshot.

And read the Bible? Trask had perused the Bible. A quote from Ecclesiastes was one of his favorites: "Vanity of vanities, saith the Preacher, All is vanity."

But wait! Trask had agreed to listen uncritically, and here he was once again focusing only on a negative interpretation. He thought about years ago, back when he was in graduate school. He had gotten a lot of positive attention and reinforcement for his ability to analytically tear apart and criticize everything he heard, read, thought, and observed. Back in those days, in that environment, there had been a big payoff for being a tough-minded cynic. But that was then, and this was now. Trask wondered if maybe it wasn't time to lighten up his attitude a little. He sighed and turned the tape back on.

Peale gave the example of a man who was afraid to ask his

boss for a raise. "Summon up your courage and ask," Peale proclaimed. "If you honestly think you deserve it. You may not get it, but you will have done wonders for your self-image, because you will have broken through the fear barrier."

Once again Trask stopped the tape. Obviously, Peale had never been a lowly employee asking for a raise. One of the surest ways to crush self-esteem is to ask for a raise and then be rejected.

Trask shook his head, hunched his shoulders and turned the tape back on. Peale quoted the poet John Milton: "The mind is its own place, and in itself can make a heaven of hell, a hell of heaven." The feeling of inferiority, said Peale, was nothing but a state of mind in nine cases out of ten.

True, thought Trask, but it wasn't Milton who said those words; it was Christopher Marlowe in his play *Dr. Faustus*.

And so it went. For every powerful positive thought and affirmation by Peale, there was an equal and opposite negation by Trask.

Both Trask and his younger brother, Tom, were too smart for their own good. Their critical, intellectual powers set up formidable barriers to recovery. They could argue convincingly that positive thinkers were shallow optimists who ignored unpleasant realities. Viewed through the finely calibrated lens of negativity, the world is hostile and human existence is, in the words of philosopher Thomas Hobbes, "solitary, poor, nasty, brutish and short." Hopeless cases? Tough, but not hopeless. It's clear that Tom and Trask live in a habitat of gloom. And sometimes it seems as though they wallow in it — they derive a peculiar form of pleasure from chronic low-grade depression.

However, Tom and Trask are well aware that their negativity undermines the quality of their lives and does nothing to enhance their relationships or any other aspect of their existence. For it is our perspective on life that sets the tone of our existence. We can look at the universe and feel an oppressive solitude at the immensity of space and the bleak and lonely isolation of our lives. Or we can echo the words of Henry David Thoreau: "Why should I feel lonely? Is not our planet in the Milky Way?"

In other words, *we can create a new vision of ourselves and our lives.*

Chapter Eleven

Creating a New Vision

If family or friends have repeatedly worried that you often seem moody, grim, dour, critical — or, more bluntly speaking, that you are a wet blanket — then odds are you suffer from habitual negativity.

Now, we humans are strange creatures. Even when we're surrounded by massive confirmatory evidence of our mugwumpish outlook on life, we have the natural tendency to raise up our hackles and growl, "Not me! There's nothing wrong with the way *I* look at the world. I see things exactly as they are. It's you guys with the rose-colored glasses who're all mixed up. So, leave me alone."

Lenny was a hard-looking lawyer. He seldom smiled. He stalked down the courthouse halls with his shoulders hunched and his face set in a doleful scowl. The few friends who were close to him had mentioned to Lenny that he had the uncanny knack of spreading dejection and gloom wherever he went.

"They told me I looked fiercely unhappy," Lenny says. "They said people were afraid to talk with me because I was sarcastic, or because they thought I was making fun of them with my biting wit."

This was brought home to Lenny when he attended the annual bar convention. As he was leaving the men's room, Lenny looked up and noticed a frowning, mean-looking guy striding straight toward him. Startled by the fellow's fierce demeanor, Lenny stepped aside to let him pass. The taciturn stranger also stepped aside. Only then did Lenny realize that he was dodging his own image in a full-length mirror.

Into the Twilight Zone

A mirror can reflect our outward image, but what about our inner image? What about the thoughts that make up our perspective on the world?

One way to find out for sure whether or not you are a habitually negative thinker is to record the thoughts that run through your mind when it shifts into the twilight zone, right before you go to sleep at night and first thing in the morning when you wake up.

It is at these two particular times of the day — when we are not fully awake, but not asleep, either — that our emotional defenses are at their lowest. We are in a twilight state, and during these twilight moments the door between our conscious and unconscious mind is not closed as tightly as usual. The fantasies and thoughts that emerge at this time can be used as powerful tools to help us understand our most basic beliefs, fears, and vulnerabilities. By recording these thoughts and fantasies, we can tune in to the deep negative beliefs and emotions that keeps our depression active.

Becoming aware of our late night and early morning cognitions is extremely important. Why? Because, without being aware of what we're doing, we virtually hypnotize ourselves with our own thoughts and fantasies. At the vulnerable moments of pre- and post-sleep, our unconscious minds are unusually receptive to suggestions.

If, at these moments, our thoughts are full of pain, betrayal, and failure, these messages will sink into our unconscious thinking to color our entire outlook on life. Automatic negative thoughts will create within us a hopeless and despairing vision of ourselves. But, by tapping into the depths of the unconscious mind, we can create a powerful new vision of ourselves as happy, peaceful, and healthy people.

The Power of Positive Images

Our plan is to:

1. Recognize our current negative pre- and post-sleep cognitions.
2. Create a set of new, powerful, positive cognitions.
3. Gently slide our new cognitions into the deep layers of our consciousness.

Our goal is to create a new vision of ourselves as happy, healthy, and positive people. Regardless of how successful we are by objective standards, we will not feel good about ourselves unless we can visualize ourselves in a positive way.

On the other hand, if we possess a positive self-image, personal setbacks cannot destroy our self-esteem. It is our *mental vision* of ourselves that determines whether we value and respect ourselves or loathe our entire existence.

Now, STOP! Before you read any further, get a piece of paper and a pencil.

Okay, ready? If you're like most people, you have a secret fantasy life that no one else knows about. The content of our fantasies can have a tremendous impact on how we feel about ourselves and our place in the world. The purpose of this exercise is to write out some of the fantasies and thoughts that run through your mind at pre- and post-sleep times.

A word of reassurance: Many of us have fantasies that are, well . . . weird. We don't want other people to know about them because we recognize — on a conscious, intellectual, adult level — that our thoughts are, well . . . weird.

Don't worry. Bizarre and childish fantasies of power, heroics, betrayal, and destruction are more common than you think. Even presidents have known lust in their hearts. As long as you don't act out your weird fantasy in real life, you have no reason to feel guilty or ashamed of yourself.

Remember, this exercise is for you. You don't have to reveal your private fantasies to anyone else in order to use them for your benefit. After writing out your fantasies and thoughts and analyzing them, you can tear up your papers and burn them if you want. But it is important that you analyze your twilight thoughts in the cold light of broad daylight so you can become aware of the negative content that you use to reinforce your negative self-image.

Okay, right now, while you are wide awake and alert, think about your pre- and post-sleep thoughts. Write down what you remember thinking right before you drift off to sleep (or when you lie awake brooding) and when you first wake up. Don't worry about grammar, style, or spelling. Let your stream of consciousness flow.

From Tom's list:

There's no such thing as an ordinary day. Every day has its own particular brand of crap you've got to eat. Every day is another bite. Every day is a crisis. Especially bad in the morning. It's the worst time of the day.

My first thought: Oh, God, not another one. Stomach tightens up. I think, where's it all gonna end? Then I yell at my kid, "Get that cat out of here!" Then I think, that fascist fool in my social problems class is going to argue with me. There's one of those jerks in every class who ruins every day. I fantasize about an instrument. I'm lying in bed with my face in the pillow and what I need is a giant blade to cut off my hands and my head simultaneously. Allie brings me a cup of coffee, and I say, "It never gets any better. It's just another frigging day." I listen to the news, lying in bed brooding about how the whole world's going to hell. Agonized feeling in my stomach when I realize its morning and I have to face another day. I talk to Allie and say over and over again, "I can't stand it anymore." I groan to myself, "Oh, God. Oh, God."

A lot of times, it's like I want to sit and half close my eyes and pretend I'm just withdrawn from everything — looking for a way to be comatose without being blamed for it so I wouldn't have to feel, wouldn't have to be around all the problems.

I feel like I'm in a grim machine that poisons my system. I'm always supposed to be doing something, writing, accomplishing. No matter what I do it's not enough. I am corroded with guilt. I can't enjoy doing anything for pleasure because I know I should be accomplishing more in my work.

My situation is the worst because there is nobody like me to relate to. Nobody can understand me. I feel overwhelmed and I have no one to talk to about what's going on in my life. I need a person who will "know" what I'm feeling without me having to explain it all. I want someone who I can sit around and talk to and who will just agree with me.

Whew! All of that before breakfast. If we accept the idea that our cognitions create our feelings, it certainly comes as no surprise that Tom feels low-down, hopeless, and depressed much of the time.

If right now, while you're awake, you're unable to recall what you think about before and after sleeping, try this: Put a pad and a pencil near your bed. At night, after you've laid in bed a few minutes, take a minute to write down the thoughts that have been running through your mind. If you sleep alone, this doesn't pose too big a problem. But if you share your bed with a partner, it's probably not a good idea to keep bouncing up and down to the light switch fifteen times in a row. Make your own notes, but please be considerate. In the morning, let your automatic thoughts flow, then STOP! Write them down. If you're pressed for time, put down just a sentence or two that captures the flavor of your early morning attitude.

Do this for several days in a row so that you can catch the pattern of your thinking.

Culturally Reinforced Fantasies

We usually develop a pattern to our fantasies — in other words, while the set and supporting characters may change, our role and the plot stays pretty much the same.

For example, Sheila, a 37-year-old public health administrator, had lulled herself to sleep with the same romantic fantasy since she was about twelve years old. Sometimes the male lead in her fantasy would be a man she really knew, while other times it would be an actor or a rock star, but it was always someone unattainable.

The plot line was always the same. Sheila would meet her fantasy man at a time when he was in great trouble or peril. He was desperate. Sheila, through great generosity and personal sacrifice, would pull him through the crisis. Their love would bloom, then disaster. As soon as her lover was back on his feet, he left her, but not before he had sexually humiliated her.

After giving her all, she was betrayed and abandoned, left with nothing but public ridicule and a broken heart. Many times, Sheila visualized herself wasting away into a wraith-like apparition, a figure of pity who aroused a strange sort of awe in onlookers.

How could one person love so much? How could she stand such pain and live? Her suffering reached such legendary proportions that it inspired both admiration and shame in all who beheld her.

These fantasies, sort of a continuing soap opera, had continued for almost 25 years. And in all those years, Sheila had never acknowledged or revealed the content of her fantasy life, not even while she was in psychotherapy. No one who knew this capable and strong woman would ever suspect that she privately pictured herself as an abused victim.

But look at the pattern in Sheila's personal soap opera:

First, she is the hero — kind, generous, powerful, and willing to sacrifice herself for the benefit of a loved one.

Second, she is the victim — used, betrayed, and abandoned.

Third, she is the martyr — her life is destroyed, yet she rises up to become a living symbol of sacrificial love and suffering.

Now listen, because this is important: The pattern of Sheila's lifelong fantasy — heroics, followed by victimization and martyrdom — is a culturally reinforced message that many, *many,* **many** women have internalized without being consciously aware of it.

Now, listen some more: If your private fantasies include similar elements, then you, too, have probably internalized this powerful cultural message.

Look at the pattern of Sheila's cognitions. Compare it to your own twilight thoughts. In the end, it was through her martyrdom to love and pain that Sheila received recognition. How could one person endure so much pain and live? It was through her martyrdom (translate to read: depression) that Sheila achieved recognition as a special person.

And what is the greatest martyrdom of all? Death, of course. Not surprisingly, Sheila had thoughts of suicide more than once.

In everyday life, Sheila strives toward personal and professional competence in all that she does. Yet, her successes do little to raise her level of self-esteem. By all objective criteria, she should feel good about herself because, by objective standards, she is a success.

Yet, Sheila's recurring fantasies clearly indicate that she has internalized the idea that it is her misery — her ability to suffer — that makes her special.

In short, her self-esteem is based on martyrdom and suffering. She hypnotizes herself every night into believing that her depressive moods set her apart from other people in a special and superior way.

The danger for Sheila and many others is this: On a subconscious level, we believe if we give up our depression, we will no longer be special. We are defined by our depression.

So, when we attempt to conquer our depression we are faced with a difficult decision. Do we choose *ordinary happiness* . . . or do we maintain the illusion that we are special by virtue of our misery?

How do we reach down into our unconscious minds and rid ourselves of the destructive cultural message that tells us our emotional pain is both necessary and good?

Drowning Out the Noise of Your Habitual Negativity

The task of reaching your unconscious mind will be much easier if you have a cassette tape recorder. You don't need a superduper deluxe model. The discount store plastic special will do just fine as long as it has an automatic shut-off and an earphone attachment.

You will also need a tape filled with inspirational and positive messages. You can either make your own tape or you can purchase a prerecorded one. Most large bookstores have racks of motivational, hypnotic, and subliminal tapes on a variety of subjects.

If you purchase a tape, pick one with a title such as: "Be More Positive," "Learn to Relax," or "Raising Self-Esteem." These tapes usually contain a series of soothing suggestions and soft background music. The inexpensive tapes seem just as good as expensive ones, so unless you have money to burn, you don't have to pay a lot to get a good product.

If you want to make your own tape, you might record quotations from inspirational books (such as *The Prophet* by Kahlil Gibran) or pertinent Bible passages. You'll need at least 30 minutes of positive messages.

Okay, this is our plan: For years, you have been "hypnotizing" yourself with negative, painful, and destructive messages during the moments of pre- and post-sleep when your unconscious mind is most vulnerable to suggestion. Now, use the cassette player and your tape of positive suggestions to drown out the noise of your negative thoughts.

Our goal is to saturate our minds with positive thoughts.

During the pre- and post sleep moments when your unconscious mind is open to suggestion, you're going to give yourself a big dose of positive thinking. The neat thing is that you don't have to actively do anything except turn on the cassette player and fall asleep listening to positive messages instead of to the noise of your own negativity.

Plug the tape recorder in next to your bed. Either use an earphone, or put the recorder close enough to your head so you can hear the message with the volume on low. You don't want to blast the whole house down! All you have to do now is fall asleep listening to the tape. If negative, upsetting thoughts invade your mind, gently say to yourself, "Stop. I'm not going to think about that now." Then focus your attention back on the sound of the tape. If you awake during the night with your mind racing with disturbing thoughts, listen to the tape again.

A word of caution: Please be sure to arrange your cassette player and its various cords carefully so you don't entangle yourself if you roll over in your sleep. Some people prefer to use an inexpensive machine they can place under their pillow. If the machine is knocked out of bed, there's usually no damage.

Your habit of negativity may make you doubt such a simple little exercise could be helpful. But what do you have to lose? Try it every night for a month. When you go to sleep at night, turn on the cassette (use an earphone if you sleep with a partner who doesn't want to listen) and fall asleep to the positive messages. You don't even have to try to stay awake until the tape is over. The message will go right into your unconscious mind as you sleep.

When you wake up in the morning, turn on the positive tape again and listen to it as you get ready to meet the day. Remember, our purpose is to block out the habitual negativity while saturating our minds with new, positive thoughts.

After using this technique for 30 days, try an experiment. Get out your pencil and paper again and record your night and morning thoughts. Do you see a difference? Almost everyone we know who has tried this technique finds their automatic thoughts are shifting away from gloom and doom and toward hope and happiness.

Sheila said, "I still have fantasies, but I'm no longer playing the role of the martyred victim. For the first time in 25 years I'm not picturing myself as rejected and abandoned all the time. I realize now where these fantasies came from. When I was twelve, my parents had a lot a problems in their marriage. I tried everything I could to fix things up between them, but it didn't work out. They didn't get divorced, but we were never a family after that. I felt really alone and betrayed and unloved. I wanted them to know how much they had hurt me. I guess I've been punishing them — and myself — ever since. But slowly, my self-image is changing as I listen to my positive thinking tapes. I'm beginning to feel a lot closer to my husband — I guess I'm no longer looking for evidence of rejection. He's noticed the change in me, too. He says I'm easier to be around. My whole attitude seems to be changing for the better."

An interesting note: One of the symptoms of depression is lack of motivation. Sometimes we feel so overwhelmed that we don't know where we will get the energy to do one more thing. That's why using a cassette player and a tape of positive thoughts is custom-made for us. It requires very little motivation and energy. One trip to the bookstore for a tape — one tape is enough, so we don't have to make a decision every night about which one to listen to.

Plug in your tape player by the bed and leave it there. All you have to do is turn on the player and occasionally flip the tape over. Easy. There's nothing more to *do*, you just *be*, as a soothing voice guides you into a deep state of relaxation where your unconscious mind can accept positive messages.

Come on, give it a try for 30 days. You may be pleasantly surprised at how a "new" you emerges, a you with a more hopeful and positive outlook on life.

Chapter Twelve

Guilt

Rori's Story

Rori felt so depressed she could hardly drag herself out of bed to go to work. She faced each day with apprehension. Yet, she couldn't call in sick, she couldn't take time off. She had to be there. Had to. More than once these past few weeks she had thought to herself, if things get any worse, I might as well end it all.

Since her divorce from Bill, Rori worked as a bookkeeper in a doctor's office. Her afternoons and evenings were spent alone or at the shopping malls. She'd been in limbo for months, waiting for something to happen, and shopping seemed to break the monotony.

But now something was about to break, and Rori was scared. *Scared* — the word didn't begin to describe what she was feeling. She was filled with guilt and frightened out of her wits. She couldn't even work up enough spit to swallow.

Later that day, brooding and smoking a Marlboro, Rori sat at a small table in a restaurant that opened onto the mall. "It isn't like I committed a crime," she tried to reassure herself. "It's like a loan. I'm not a crook." She fully intended to pay back all the money she'd borrowed from the cash receipts at work, but every month she was short. She just didn't have the money, she thought, to live decently. That was Bill's fault. Ever since the divorce, she never had enough money.

At first, she had only dipped into the petty cash, fixing it with fake receipts. Then she got behind in her car payments, and all that money was right there in front of her — why did some patients insist on paying in cash? Didn't they know checks were safer? Rori had tinkered with the books and taken — no, *borrowed* — $212, just enough for her car payment, not a penny more. "I'll pay it back," she told herself. "It's just a short-term loan." The small self-deceit soon mushroomed into a waking nightmare.

The next month, there'd been more bills, more demanding letters from creditors. One thing led to another, and now she owed the doctor more than $10,000. She knew he'd treat her like a common thief if he found out what she'd done.

That word — *thief* — had been on her mind for a long time. It had been eating at her until she thought she'd go crazy. That's why she did that stupid thing with the lottery tickets. She had felt real optimistic about it. Old Mr. Henderson had come in and paid off his bill in cash — over $800 — and Rori had seen her opportunity. She didn't have to worry about getting caught because the old man had come in at lunchtime when no one else was in the office. So Rori had taken the money and bought $800 worth of lottery tickets. She would hit a big one, the odds were in her favor, then she'd pay back all the money she had borrowed from the accounts and have some left over for herself.

She'd felt so excited, almost maniac with anticipation, as she scratched away at the tickets looking for the big winner. She wanted to sing and dance, thinking her troubles would all be over soon. *Like hell.* Out of an $800 investment in the lottery, she realized a $92 return. That was two months ago. She hadn't paid back a dime, and the doctor was beginning to get suspicious. Late yesterday afternoon she'd found him going over the accounts. He looked up, glaring at her, then without saying a word, he turned around and stomped away.

Rori crushed out her cigarette and immediately lit another. If her family found out about what she'd done, they'd never forgive her. Her mother would probably kill her! Once, when Rori was about nine, she had been caught stealing a candy bar from the grocery store. Her mother had just about gone crazy.

"Do you want to go to jail?" her mother had screamed. "Do you want to disgrace the whole family? Huh? Do you?"

She'd grabbed Rori by the shoulders, shaking her back and forth, and Rori had blubbered in fear and shame. Even now Rori felt the fear clutching at her belly, felt the shame gnawing away deep inside her. Guilt overwhelmed her. How could she have been so stupid? Her parents had taught her the difference between right and wrong. Why had she taken those first few dollars? Her mother was going to die when she found out.

She tried to brush the image of her mother out of her mind, something she could easily do when she was feeling okay, but not now. Now, Rori could barely breathe. She felt as if a huge weight was crushing her down, smashing her flat. Oh, God, what was she going to do? How was she ever going to pay back the money? If they caught her, would she have to go to jail? Why couldn't she just stop breathing? That would make things so much easier. Why couldn't she just disappear?

Guilt. It has been called the battery acid of the soul. It can corrode our self-esteem and burn a hole through the veneer of our serenity. But guilt is not all bad because the chief cause of guilt is wrongdoing. We only feel guilty when we have violated our sense of what is right and wrong. Guilt is a signal for us to examine our behavior and clean it up if it's not consistent with our values.

When we do something morally wrong, we get a guilty conscience. This is a normal and natural occurrence. Unfortunately, a guilty conscience makes us feel like hell. So, we naturally want to do whatever we can to make ourselves feel better.

Too often, though, we attempt to deal with our bad feelings by trying to silence our conscience rather than by examining and changing our behavior.

Getting Caught

Sometimes it's not the immorality of our behavior that causes our anguish, but the fear of being found out. If we have lied or cheated or stolen and gotten away with it, we can sometimes forget our guilty feelings for a while. Yet, if we are in danger of being discovered, our buried guilt feelings burst to the surface like a resurrected corpse in one of George Romero's *Living Dead* movies, and we're thrown into a state of agitated panic.

When this kind of guilt hits, watch out! Rori, the young woman who embezzled money from her employer, had been able to semi-stifle her conscience for months. She had successfully reinterpreted her theft by calling it a loan and by telling herself she fully intended to pay it back with interest. The good intentions and small deceits worked to quiet her conscience . . . until she realized her boss was on to her scheme. Suddenly, the truth of her wrongdoing slapped her in the face, changing her instantly from a calm embezzler into a terrified little girl blubbering with fear. All of her rationalizations about borrowing and paying back the money collapsed around her.

Rori was in big trouble and she didn't see any way out. No way except magic or suicide. Again and again the insistent thought came, if only I could disappear. . . .

We are in the greatest danger of doing something dangerous and foolish when we realize we are about to be caught. The dread of punishment combined with the humiliation of having to face family and friends can drive us to the edge of despair. Many of us think we would rather die than be found out. We don't bother to calmly weigh our alternatives — we panic!

Rori was indeed in big trouble. There's no denying that. But her situation was not as hopeless as she believed it to be. She had options — difficult and unpleasant ones to be sure — but options nonetheless.

Now, listen: NO SITUATION IS HOPELESS. It may be

unpleasant, dangerous, and frightening, but if we face it head-on, we have the chance of salvaging something positive out of disaster. We must call upon our grit and face our mistakes and, where possible, make amends. When we can't right our wrongs, what we can do is make the best of a bad situation. Adding new trouble on top of old trouble doesn't solve anything.

We can get ourselves into some terrible predicaments and think we have no way out. So, we deal with the situation in destructive ways — which only makes matters worse.

Some people try to lose themselves in alcohol or other drugs. The old joke says the conscience dissolves in alcohol. But when the effects of the drug wear off, we awaken to find we have not vanquished guilt, we have only taken time out. We have not lost ourselves — we have lost time.

Other people withdraw into depression or physical illness. There's a great temptation to crawl into a dark room, pull the covers over our heads, and assume the fetal position.

Still others run away, leaving their job or family or city behind. This is sometimes called *the geographic cure*.

The most desperate people attempt suicide. Many impulsive suicidal attempts are made in the panic stage of guilt. We may actually intend to kill ourselves, or we may be trying to scare the people around us so they won't go so hard on us when they find out our guilty secrets.

So, here we are. We have done something bad and we're about to be discovered. In short, the jig is up. We don't know which way to turn. Our insides are self-destructing and we dread facing the consequences of our behavior. What a mess!

The following people found themselves in just such a fix:

Sixteen-year-old Pam discovered she was pregnant. How could she tell her strict Catholic parents that the father of he baby could be any one of four different guys?

Brian was such a promising student that his parents had mortgaged their home to raise the money to send him to Stanford. But competition at the university was tough and

Brian couldn't hack it. He registered but had skipped most of his classes and had flunked out. His parents, still unaware of his failure, want to see his grades.

Angela had promised her husband she would curtail her credit card shopping until they got their old bills paid off. But her cousin had gotten married and there had been her sister's birthday and her best friend's baby shower. She'd had to buy gifts, and maybe she had gone overboard, but she didn't want to look cheap. Now, the creditors were demanding payment and threatening court action. She couldn't hide the bills any longer. What was she going to do?

Pastor Smith had never intended his flirtation with Mrs. Johnson to end up in a motel room, but it had. When he tried to break off the relationship, she threatened a lawsuit against him and promised to tell his wife and the entire congregation exactly what kind of man he really was.

As part of her job as office manager for a small, private social service agency, Jennifer was supposed to file monthly employee tax reports with both the state and federal revenue departments. She had gotten behind. And she'd started getting these threatening letters from the IRS demanding an immediate response or else. She'd hidden the letters from her boss, but she still hadn't gotten around to filing the reports. Now, the IRS was threatening to padlock the doors and seize assets if the accounts weren't cleared within fourteen days. There was no way she could do it without asking her boss for assistance, but to do that she'd have to admit she had really screwed up and then lied to save face. She'd probably get fired and never be able to get another job once the word got out about what she had done.

When We Don't Get Caught but We Still Feel Guilty

Sometimes our misbehavior goes undetected, but this is no guarantee we will get off free. Wrongdoing damages our self-esteem. Our guilty conscience prevents us from liking ourselves.

As we said before, we will feel guilty whenever we violate the conscious or unconscious rules by which we live. Whenever we violate these rules — whether the rules make sense or not — our inner voice says we deserve to be punished. And if we are not punished by outside forces, we will punish ourselves with feelings of inferiority, ill health, personal failure, poor performance, anxiety, or deep feelings of depression.

Sometimes our guilty feelings are irrational. We can be decent, well-meaning people and still be overwhelmed with feelings of guilt and remorse over our failure to live up to impossibly high standards of perfect behavior. This kind of guilt is often vague and insidious, filling us with a profoundly disturbing sense of not only doing bad, but of *being* bad. Most depressed people suffer from this kind of vague, irrational guilt at one time or another.

Because irrational guilt is based on failure to behave perfectly, rather than on actually behaving badly, it serves no good purpose. Practicing the *Changing the Rules* exercise in Chapter Eight can help us overcome irrational guilt.

But at other times our guilt is totally rational, as in Rori's case. She feels guilty because she *is* guilty. She has done something bad — taken money that doesn't belong to her and lied to cover her tracks. Now that she is about to be discovered, she is suffering from much guilt and despair.

Guilt, whether it is rational or irrational, can be a great stress producer. As Rori sat in the restaurant smoking cigarettes and brooding about getting caught, certain biochemical reactions were taking place in her body. When she thought, oh, God, I might go to jail — her body responded with a panic reaction. Adrenaline poured into her bloodstream, followed by glucose, insulin, and many other body chemicals. Her heart started beating fast, she had trouble breathing, her bowels rumbled, her skin crawled. This was not an isolated reaction, not a split-second wave of distress that vanished after a few moments. She'd been in a quiet panic for weeks. Day after day her guilty thoughts fueled the panic response in her body. After awhile, her biochemistry was thoroughly unbalanced, and Rori developed the classic symptoms of a biochemical depression.

Guilt, then, can be both a symptom and a cause of depression.

While medication might ease the severity of some of Rori's worst symptoms — insomnia, choking sensations, preoccupation with dying, dry vomiting, nightmares, and so on — she needs more than medical intervention to recover from her terrible depression. She needs *moral intervention.*

Moral Intervention

If we are to break depression's steely grip on our psyche, it is mandatory that we bring our behavior into alignment with our vision of the kind of person we would like to be.

We cannot be happy, healthy, competent, loved, and respected people if we don't act that way.

We cannot be happy when we are filled with guilt.

We cannot be healthy if we abuse our bodies with alcohol or other drugs, or if we have poor living habits or a wild life-style.

We cannot become competent if we hide whenever we are faced with adversity.

We cannot find love if we abuse or reject the people who care about us.

And we cannot be respected if we are liars or frauds who cheat or steal.

We're not talking about trying to live up to some impossible, childish fantasy of omnipotent perfection here. We're not talking about sainthood or becoming a moral paragon. We're talking about living up to a realistic vision of ourselves as moral people.

Peter, a 39-year-old social worker, was prescribed antidepressant medication after an exhausting series of medical tests turned up blank. "I don't know what I'm depressed about," he complained. "I just know I feel awful and I dread each new day." For a long time he had been suffering insomnia and had a tightness in his chest and a feeling of light-headedness. Sometimes he had trouble catching his breath. Worst of all was a horrible cloud of doom that hovered over him all the time — it was like something awful was about to happen any minute. Every time the phone rang, he jumped, afraid it might be news of disaster.

The medication helped — a little. He slept better, he didn't feel so dizzy, and he could breathe with less difficulty. But the cloud of doom was still there.

One night Peter called a friend in a real panic. "What's happened?" the friend asked.

"I don't know," he said desperately. "But I feel really bad. The pills aren't working anymore. I'm terribly depressed. I just can't stand myself. I feel totally worthless. I'm useless. I don't know why I feel this way, but I do. I can't stand it."

As Peter talked on, it became clear he did know why he was feeling so low, but he didn't want to admit it, not even to himself. In a nutshell, Peter had shattered his self-esteem by steadily violating his basic code of ethics. He had tried to convince himself he could part company with his basic moral values without having to suffer any unpleasant consequences.

He was wrong.

Peter, a married man with two young children, had been carrying on an affair with a married co-worker for over a year. The affair itself created guilty feelings in Peter. But Peter's guilt was intensified by the fact that he made his living as a marriage and family counselor. He was also a popular conference speaker on the subject of honesty in relationships. It was no wonder Peter was full of guilt-ridden conflicts, anxiety, and depression.

Here he was, presenting a public image of himself as a caring and honest family man, when in reality he was living an absolute lie. His behavior was in total contradiction to everything he stood for. At any moment he could be found out, unmasked as a liar and a fraud. Is it any surprise he dreaded the ringing of the telephone?

There was more: He drank too much and he smoked marijuana. He lied to his wife about money, and he paid for some of his weekend romances with his agency's credit card.

Peter considered himself to be a decent and moral person — and he was. Had he been any different, he could have lied and cheated without a twinge of guilt. But his ingrained decency haunted him. How could he like himself, how could he relax, how could he be happy when every single day he violated his higher values? His depression, fear, and anxiety were the punishments handed down by his guilty conscience.

Once he admitted his guilt to himself and made efforts to rectify his wrongdoing, Peter's cloud of gloom and doom vanished. It wasn't easy. He had to make some hard decisions about how he wanted to live. He had to give up some pleasurable things. But he gained back a measure of serenity by bringing his behavior into closer alignment with his values. Peter no longer needed to punish himself with depression and self-hate.

Do Right, Feel Right

Could the same be true for you? Have you been violating your higher values with dishonesty, scheming, or cheating? Is it possible that your depression could be the revenge of an exacting conscience?

Now is the time for a searching moral inventory. Ask yourself if you are living up to your higher values.

If the answer is "no," are you willing to examine your behavior and make the necessary changes?

This is no easy task. It takes time and patience, and it can be painful. You may have fallen so far off the path that you believe you are beyond redemption.

Listen: No situation is so hopeless that a solution cannot be found. We can overcome our mistakes and make a new start.

But the reality is this: If we have messed up in some way, if we really have done something bad, then we have to pay the consequences, which will almost always include:

- personal embarrassment;
- enduring the anger and disapproval of other people;
- making amends;
- accepting punishment;
- forgiving ourselves for our mistakes and forgiving the people who have hurt us.

We can deliver ourselves from the tyranny of guilt, but we must remember we can't just *think right* while continuing to *do wrong*. Saying, "I'm sorry," then going out and committing the same moral errors again won't wash. To feel right, we have to start doing right.

Now let's move on to some step-by-step suggestions on how to break free from the guilt trap without compromising or abandoning our higher values.

Chapter Thirteen

Guilt-Busters

How you go about clearing your guilty conscience — and the accompanying feelings of low self-esteem and depression — depends a great deal on what you have done wrong. Guilt comes in varying degrees, and we must deal with it in different ways.

First Degree Guilt: Indictable Offenses

The most frightened, despairing, guilt-ridden people are the ones who are usually law-abiding and respectable, but who have gotten themselves involved in some law-breaking scam or scheme. We're not talking about hardened criminals here — you know, the kind of guys who can do two years in the slammer resting on their elbows.

No, we're talking about a basically moral person who, for whatever reason, has broken the law and is lying in bed at night visualizing all the terrible consequences bound to happen when he or she gets caught. This kind of guilt can create so much agitated fear and depression that people lose the ability to think and act in a rational fashion.

Because we are frightened and ashamed, we keep our guilt secret from everyone else. A knock on the door or the ring of a phone can put us into a frenzy of fear or turn us into emotional zombies. To cover our tracks we lie, manipulate and cover-up, and, naturally, all of this dishonesty makes us feel even more guilty.

What sort of criminal offenses do respectable people commit?

- Sandra continued to write checks on a closed checking account.
- Bill continued to drive after his driver's license was suspended.
- Phyllis smashed into another car in a parking lot and drove away.
- David turned in a phony insurance claim.
- Patty found someone's long distance telephone credit card and used it to make calls all over the country.
- Edward, a business executive, used insider's knowledge to make a killing on the stock market.
- Sheila, a minister's daughter, sold cocaine and marijuana from her college dorm room in order to earn extra spending money.

So, what does a person who is involved in shady dealings do? How do we make things right?

1. *Face the music*. The first step is to sit down, take a deep breath, and face the music. Carefully analyze the entire situation and your part in it. Be brutally honest with yourself. Accept no excuses. You are a moral person and you know the difference between right and wrong. If you have behaved dishonestly, come right out and admit it to yourself.

This step is vital because it allows you to start dealing with the situation realistically from here on out. You have been using rationalizations and excuses to justify your actions and this has blurred your judgment and allowed your mistakes to pile up one on top of the other. So, be absolutely honest in your analysis. Self-honesty will at least give you a clear perspective on where to go from here.

2. *Stop the behavior*. Whatever illegal or immoral act you have been committing, STOP IT! Right now. Stop writing bad checks, stop selling drugs, stop driving while suspended, stop taking money that doesn't belong to

you. There's always a part of us that doesn't want to stop, for whatever reason — sometimes because of ambivalence ("I know I should stop, but . . . well, I'll quit tomorrow."), or perhaps because of sheer ornery cussedness ("No one's going to tell me how to live my life!").

Accept no excuses! Issue a Cease and Desist order on yourself. You cannot free yourself from guilt and depression as long as you continue your wrongdoing.

What if you have tried, honestly tried, and you cannot stop? Some behaviors — such as shoplifting, drug-related or sex-related activities, or gambling — can become compulsions. This means you have lost the ability to control yourself in this area. If you have tried to stop committing acts which are illegal, self-destructive, or harmful to others, and you have failed, you need professional help. Do not delay any longer. Seek the help of your doctor, a counselor, psychologist or psychiatrist.

3. *Consult the experts.* If you are involved in illegal activities or shady deals, you would also be wise to seek the counsel of experts who are qualified to help people in trouble, and who will keep the troubles confidential. Talk to a lawyer to find out what your rights and obligations are. If you have money or tax problems, see a reputable accountant. Get the facts from someone who knows what they're talking about, not from someone who has as little experience as you do.

Craig, a self-employed carpenter, had not filed tax returns for five years. He was terrified of what was going to happen once the IRS caught up with him. He even turned down good paying work with a contractor who filed monthly IRS statements. The worry, guilt, and fear over his taxes generated so much anxiety and depression in Craig that he felt as if his life was coming apart.

Although Craig was under tremendous pressure from worrying about the IRS, he was in therapy for seven months before he even mentioned the subject of his taxes. His therapist instructed him to immediately contact an accounting service that specialized in income taxes.

Craig resisted. "It won't do any good. I don't have any records. They'll turn me in to the IRS and I'll go to federal prison. Why can't you help me?"

"Because I'm a counselor, not a tax consultant," his therapist replied. "I don't know any more about the tax code than you do. You need expert help, and in this case I'm not it."

Reluctantly, Craig consulted a tax expert. It took six months and a second mortgage on his house, but Craig did get himself straight with the IRS. He wasn't indicted and he didn't go to jail. But he did have to pay a substantial tax penalty and a fee to the consultant. To his amazement, most of his unpleasant emotional symptoms cleared up as soon as he had the IRS off his trail.

There are two morals to be drawn from Craig's case:

Sometimes we need expensive expert help to get ourselves out of trouble. We're foolish if we avoid it because we're embarrassed or we don't want to spend the money. If you don't know where to find expert help, a counselor, minister, or a wise friend can sometimes help you analyze your options.

Some of us spend hours and hours in therapy trying to find ways to feel better without confronting our indictable offense. We would like the worrisome guilt and depression to go away without having to change our act. And some of us would prefer to be crazy or have a brain tumor rather than admit we are scared to death because we're in danger of having our illegal or immoral activities catch up with us.

4. *Take the consequences.* Be prepared to make amends and to accept some unpleasant consequences. Too often we hope we can get away with a slap on the wrist and a promise not to be bad anymore. That might have worked when we were children, but it won't do now. To get yourself right — to clear your conscience — you

may have to make sacrifices, financially and emotionally. You have to put time and energy into creating solutions. And you have to swallow your PRIDE.

Some illegal activities are considered to be victimless crimes — driving while suspended, for instance. If the behavior you feel guilty about has not harmed anyone else, it is enough that you STOP IT! Once you stop acting like a criminal, you'll stop feeling like one.

But what does someone like Sandra, who wrote bad checks, do? She's in a real jam because . . .

- She cheated a number of individuals and businesses out of money.
- It's only a matter of time before the authorities catch up with her.
- There's a good chance that once she's caught, she'll go to jail.

Worrying about all this put Sandra into a deep depression. She was so frightened that she didn't want to leave her house. She stayed in bed, telling everyone she had the flu. (She didn't.) She kept her house dark and the shades drawn so if someone (like a cop) came to the door, they'd think she wasn't home. She even refused to open her mail or answer the phone. She was like an ostrich, trying to hide its head in the sand — except Sandra hid her head under the bed covers.

The urge to hide, hoping the unpleasant truth will somehow disappear, is extremely common among people who are prone to depression. Does this tactic work? Usually not. After all, we are amateurs in the world of crime. We almost always get caught. And if we don't, our conscience punishes us more severely than any judge would.

Sandra knew she'd get caught sooner or later. The bad checks she had written were imprinted with her name and address. So it was only a matter of time before the knock on the door was not "Avon calling," but a uniformed police officer with a warrant for her arrest.

Sandra had a choice. She could hide in her room and

wrestle with her conscience and her deepening depression while she waited to be arrested. Or she could take matters into her own hands and try to set things right.

With much fear, trepidation, and embarrassment, Sandra went to the manager of her bank and told him what she had done. She asked him to help her arrange a plan to set things right. Not surprisingly, the banker was cold and disapproving toward Sandra. He lectured her sternly, telling her many bad things she didn't want to hear about herself. But, more importantly, he agreed to help her.

"Facing that man at the bank was the most horrible, embarrassing thing I've ever had to do," Sandra said later, "but it was something I couldn't avoid if I wanted to get myself out of the fix I was in. I cried and shook, I was so scared. But it was all worth it. After I signed all the papers and agreed to make payments the way they demanded, I felt so relieved, I couldn't believe it. I walked out of there feeling like a different person. I wasn't a liar anymore. I wasn't a crook. I was a person again!"

Had Sandra not taken measures to set her wrongdoing right, she would surely have been arrested and convicted on a bad check charge. In order to pay back the money she owed, she had to go through months of scrimping and deprivation. She also had to pay a large service charge and face the embarrassment of being blacklisted at the bank. But this was a small price to be free of guilt for the first time in many months.

One could argue that Sandra's sudden conversion to doing right was merely a matter of self-preservation. Her other choice was jail. But what do you do if you've committed a misdeed, your conscience is killing you, and you were never caught? How do you make amends then?

A very depressed client named Walter confessed that a year earlier, he had pinched several hundred dollars from a fund his co-workers had collected for a local charity. No one suspected him. No one even knew the money was missing. But Walter was beside himself with guilt and self-loathing. How could he have done such a low-down, sneaky thing? Surely, God would punish him for his crime. He'd always led a religious, respectable life, and now he felt doomed to suffer because of his one moment of weakness.

Walter truly wanted to make amends, yet he was frightened. If he confessed to his boss and co-workers, he would probably lose his job, causing extreme hardship for his children. Was it fair to punish his kids for his own wrongdoing? But if he didn't clear his conscience, he might not ever be able to live with himself. He felt totally lost and helpless.

In order to make amends and get on with his life, Walter needed to return the money, pay a penance, set his moral sights straight, and make peace with his Higher Power. He decided to do several things. First, he would anonymously make a $250 contribution to a worthy charity. This would pay back the money he had taken. It was important that the gift be anonymous so Walter would receive neither personal credit nor a tax deduction.

Second, he would contribute at least 100 hours of unpaid volunteer work to a worthy cause.

Third, he would examine the moral yardstick by which he measured himself, and he would strive to live up to his higher values on a regular basis.

Fourth (and this was very important for Walter), he decided to put the problem in God's hands. He had felt so guilty about his small crime that he had turned totally away from prayer. He felt unworthy of God's love. To fully recover, Walter again had to place his faith and trust in a Power greater than himself. He asked for strength and forgiveness and he received it. Slowly, as Walter brought his behavior into alignment with his vision of himself, his depression and self-loathing vanished.

Now, let's pause for a moment. Are you suffering from a guilty conscience? Could your fear, anxiety, and depression be the result of a current or past wrongdoing? If the answer is "yes," you can set yourself straight.

1. Analyze your situation calmly and honestly. If you have done something wrong, admit it to yourself and start making plans to set yourself straight.
2. If you are currently involved in wrongdoing, STOP IT! If you can't stop on your own, seek professional help.
3. Seek the counsel and guidance of people who are qualified to help you — such as a lawyer, accountant, banker, counselor, or minister.
4. Be prepared to make personal, emotional, and financial amends to those you have hurt, and be willing to take the consequences for your wrongdoing (anger, disapproval, legal action, even jail).
5. Put the problem into the hands of your Higher Power. It is time to seek forgiveness and to forgive yourself.

Second Degree Guilt: Violations of Cultural Virtues

Although it is not against the law to lie, most of us would agree that lying is wrong. Labeling someone a liar is a true insult. Yet, can you honestly say you are not a liar?

Some lies — the socially acceptable white lies — are not so bad. They may even be kind. For instance:

"Don't be silly, dear. Of course, little Jason's ears don't make him look like a chimpanzee. He's as cute as he can be."

Or: "Oh, yes, I agree. I think painting your house deep purple does symbolize your daring individualism."

Or: "How nice, you came early."

Tactful insincerities may indeed be lies, but so what? People who go around being 100 percent truthful when expressing their opinions are not really being honest — they're being hostile. For these people, truthfulness is not a virtue. They use The Truth as a club to hurt and demean their friends.

Most of us intuitively understand the difference between the virtue of tact and the vice of plain old black lies. . . .

"How should I know who took the money out of your purse?"

"Honest, honey, I have to work late tonight."

"Don't worry, the check is in the mail."

Black lies — used to cover-up dishonesty, deceit, and irresponsibility. While these kinds of lies are not against the law, they do violate the general rules of good conduct that most people hold in high esteem. We gain a certain sense of satisfaction out of doing what is correct in our business and personal lives. If we violate our personal code of right and wrong, we suffer pangs of guilt.

Now, we hit a tricky place here. Our society holds certain values in high regard:

- honesty
- truthfulness
- loyalty
- integrity
- fairness
- kindness
- faithfulness

And so on. But we start learning at home and in school that these traits are not universally rewarded. In sports competition, we get the double message:

Play fair / Winning is everything.

The cultural purpose of the first message is to strengthen and simplify social life so that we're able to do what is basically right without having to think about it. The second message allows the individual to think more about his or her own needs and less about the feelings of others or the needs of society as a whole.

Some other incompatible messages are . . .

Be loyal to your friends / Look out for #1.

A man's word is his bond / Never give a sucker an even break.

Take care of your family / Find your own space.

Virtue is its own reward / If it feels good, do it.

Such double messages can be very confusing to us if we want to do right by others and take care of our own private needs, too. We can find ourselves in a situation where our higher values and our personal desires clash head-on. The result? Confusion, guilt, anger, and, all too often, depression.

Michelle shared her guilt feelings and depression in a women's support group. "I'm a terrible mother," she cried. "My house is a disaster area. The kids come home from school and I'm at work. My husband's always on my case because I'm such a bad homemaker. It's not fair. I know I should keep the house up better, but I work full-time and I have a right to meet my own needs, too." Michelle continued on with stories of guilt and anger over unmade beds, unwashed laundry, and the chocolate chip cookies she never had time to bake for her kids.

She received lots of support and sympathy from the other women in the group, all of whom were working wives and mothers struggling with the same pressures and guilt feelings. "There's never enough time to do everything," they all agreed. "We've got to learn to judge ourselves less harshly."

But as the weeks passed, Michelle continued to insist, "I'm a bad wife and mother." The other women tried to reason with her. "Look, Michelle," Donna said, "I've been to your house and it's cleaner than mine. You're not a bad housekeeper. Why do you keep torturing yourself by insisting you are? You're a working woman, you can't expect to have everything as perfectly spotless as a magazine advertisement. Loosen up a little, honey. You're doing okay."

"No," Michelle persisted. "I'm bad."

"You've got a real problem with low self-esteem," Anna said. And then the group offered Michelle positive feedback that they hoped would help her see herself more realistically.

The problem was Michelle did see herself realistically. When she said, "I am a bad wife and mother," she was making a perfectly accurate statement. For, you see, Michelle had been systematically violating her higher values in regard to her family and her own sense of right and wrong. And it had absolutely nothing to do with a lack of homemade chocolate chip cookies.

When a person says, "I'm bad," the first reaction of friends is to protest, "Oh, no, you aren't." We try to make them feel better by bolstering their self-esteem, but, in fact, they know themselves better than we do.

When we say, "I'm bad," we are saying quite clearly that we have behaved in a way that violates what we believe to be correct conduct. Unfortunately, most of us are too ashamed to admit exactly what we've done that upsets us so much, so we babble on about superficialities.

Michelle was not filled with self-loathing because she didn't have time to starch the family laundry. She was ravaged with guilt because:

- She polished off a pint of vodka every night between 6:00 and 9:00.
- Her unpredictable rages caused her children to cry themselves to sleep half the time.
- She was desperately trying to hide her drinking problem and the conflicts with her children from everyone, so she had to lie and make excuses all the time to the people she cared about.
- She was sleeping on the couch because she was furious with her husband for nagging her about her drinking.

Denying the Obvious

All of us come equipped with a set of built-in mental filters that allow us to ignore certain unpleasant truths about ourselves, our lives, and the people we love. For instance, a fair number of heart attack victims refuse to believe what's happening to them, even after they're hooked up to machines in the intensive care unit. "Indigestion," they insist. "A pulled muscle." Countless people die every year because they refuse to heed the warning signs of heart trouble.

The same thing is true with emotional problems. Michelle was suffering from depression, marriage problems, family problems, and personal problems. She knew her life was a mess, and she shared her pain with her women friends. But

Michelle kept the true source of her despair hidden.

The mental filter of denial kept her from admitting she drank too much, abused her children, and ignored her husband. Instead, she complained about unmade beds. A perfectly clean house could not alleviate Michelle's guilt and depression because bad housekeeping was not the cause of her guilt and despair.

Michelle was a secret alcoholic. Her mother had been an alcoholic, too. Like millions of others raised in any kind of disturbed home, Michelle grew up thinking she didn't deserve and would never be able to enjoy any of the good things life had to offer. She handled her daily frustrations with secret nighttime drinking.

After three drinks, her personality changed. She became mean-spirited and abusive, and she took her venomous feelings out on her family. So, of course she suffered guilt and rage and despair of the most torturous kind. More than once she considered suicide.

When Michelle admitted she had a drinking problem and entered treatment, she was finally able to recognize the true source of her guilt and depression. She also found she could handle the ups and downs of everyday life without crumbling or turning to alcohol and pills.

"I'm still not a perfect wife and mother," she admits candidly. "I probably never will be, but now I realize that I don't have to be perfect in order to be a good person. Back in the days before I got honest with myself, the slightest little mistake made me feel like a complete failure. Now, I'm more realistic. And since I'm not drinking and acting like a monster around my kids, I don't have so much to feel guilty about. Admitting that my drinking and my life were out of control and going into treatment were the best things I ever did. Can you believe it?" Michelle asked laughing. "*I actually like myself now!*"

Chapter Fourteen

Tuning In to the Right Signals

Getting beyond denial — admitting out loud to ourselves that we are guilty of violating our code of right and wrong — is difficult because of the jumble of incompatible cultural messages competing for our attention.

Which signals do you listen to?

The one that says you should be faithful to your spouse? Or the one that says this is the age of open marriage?

Do you commit yourself to another person? Or do you find your own space?

Do you accept the burden of family responsibility? Or do you do your own thing?

"But I want it all," cries our inner narcissistic self, "I wanna have my cake and eat it, too!" Sorry. Except in fairy tales for children, life does not work that way.

Balancing competing values is difficult under the best of circumstances, but when temptation is staring us in the face, we usually take the path to immediate pleasure. It's not until later that we listen to our protesting conscience.

Pause for a moment. Ask yourself now — Have you been living by one standard while believing in another? Are you suffering from guilt, anger, and depression because your behavior violates your higher values?

Do you believe in honesty and tell lies?

Do you value your marriage and cheat on your spouse?

Do you love your children and abuse them emotionally or physically?

Do you respect integrity and neglect to pay your debts?

Do you yearn for self-respect and have sex with people you don't care about or who don't care about you?

Do you admire self-control and overindulge in alcohol and other drugs, or binge eating?

Do you espouse high ethics and engage in shady business practices?

Do you expect your children to remain drug-free and you light up a joint or take cocaine?

If your answer to any of these questions or to similar questions is "yes," then is it any wonder you suffer from guilt and depression? Here you are, a moral person, and you are violating your own code of ethics all over the place. Your distressing feelings of guilt and despair are understandable, for you are waging a civil war inside your own mind.

There are two ways to cope with this kind of guilt. You can bring your conscience into alignment with your behavior, or you can bring your behavior into alignment with your conscience.

How do you decide what to do? One good way is to examine your value system. Exactly what human qualities do you admire most? This question can be hard to answer because you are bombarded every day with media images that can be terribly confusing. Sometimes it seems hard to tell what's right and what's wrong anymore. Perhaps some of your guilt feelings are caused by your sincere confusion about what is right, rather than by downright bad conduct.

That's why we need to examine our value system. You see, whether we are aware of it or not, most of us really do believe in corny old things like truth, justice, and the American Way. But as we grow up and move out into the competitive world of business and upward mobility, we become jaded and much too sophisticated to verbalize the cornball virtues we still secretly believe in. So, we become split, trying to live by two different sets of rules and failing to measure up to either one. No wonder we feel torn apart by despair!

What follows are several paper and pencil exercises that can help you determine the values you hold most important.

Exercise 1. Imagine you have just learned that the earth will explode in exactly 25 years. Your newborn child will be the leader who takes a contingency of earthlings to colonize a new galaxy. You will not be one of the survivors. Your job is to instill within your child a value system that will become the foundation of the new social order. Your legacy to humanity will be the values you teach your child. What are they?

Exercise 2. Certain media figures, television characters and celebrities symbolize exaggerated human virtues and character flaws. List three media images you admire most and three you admire least, and why. Sherry's list looked like this:

Admire most:

Katharine Hepburn — she's independent, outspoken, and nonconforming.

Magnum, P.I. — he dropped out from the mainstream, but he kept his integrity. He's loyal to his friends and he always comes through in the end.

The Equalizer — he quit The Firm because he couldn't stomach the work. He's now making up for his past mistakes by helping powerless people prevail against injustice.

Admire least:

Sue Ellen Ewing — she's manipulative, conniving, and weak.

Abby Ewing — she's manipulative, conniving, and strong.

The Boss on "9 to 5" — he pushes people around, uses them, and takes credit he doesn't deserve.

Interestingly, Sherry held a lucrative administrative position with a company that used high pressure and less than ethical techniques to persuade people to enter into long-term sales contracts for dubious services. The ability to manipulate and connive was essential for success in this job. Sherry hated her work but liked the money and prestige that went with it.

"That list opened my eyes," she said. "Here I was in real life acting like the fictional Abby Ewing, conniving and scheming and doing anything for a buck. I hated it. I really wanted to be more like Thomas Magnum. He wouldn't let money cloud his integrity. Do you think Katharine Hepburn would stick to a job she hated? Would the Equalizer talk a little old lady into signing away her life savings? I had some serious thinking to do about my life."

This exercise helped Sherry realize that the requirements of her job violated her higher values. This knowledge helped her make the tough decision to give up the high-paying job she hated and take the risk of forging a new career that matched her higher values. "It was hard, really hard," Sherry said later. "But I decided I couldn't keep doing work that made me hate myself. The price I paid in peace of mind was far greater than the salary I earned. I had to make some pretty big financial sacrifices, but at least now I can stand to look at myself in the mirror."

Exercise 3. A friend named Mary explained this trick. Whenever she questioned whether what she was doing was right or wrong, she imagined her actions printed in bold type on the front page of the local newspaper.

DIVORCED MOTHER HAS SEX WITH HER BOY-FRIEND ON THE LIVING ROOM COUCH WHILE HER CHILDREN LISTEN FROM THEIR BEDROOMS

SOCIAL WORKER SEEN DRUNK AT MALE STRIP CLUB

MARY SMITH YELLS OBSCENITIES AT CHILDREN SELLING SCHOOL CANDY DOOR-TO-DOOR

If the imaginary headlines make Mary cringe in shame, she

knows her actions are not in keeping with her higher values.

On the other hand, some of her imaginary headlines might be a little embarrassing, but not shameful. This is behavior she can live with (even though she really wouldn't want to see it on the front page of the newspaper).

GRADUATE OF ST. LEO'S CATHOLIC GIRLS' SCHOOL GOES ON THE PILL

THIRTY-YEAR-OLD WOMAN REFUSES TO GO HOME TO MOTHER'S FOR CHRISTMAS

These exercises can help you recognize the values you hold in highest esteem. If you don't like what you see, you can work to change your values into something you can respect. And if you uncover some dusty old beliefs you can be proud of, blow off the cobwebs and start living up to them again!

Letting Go

One of life's great tragedies is the fact that sometimes we cannot make amends for our past mistakes. It is too late. The child we neglected is grown and gone, the parent we ignored is dead, the lover we lied to now loves someone else. If we could, we would turn back the clock and make everything different . . . but we can't.

Regret torments us. Our depression lingers on because we can't — won't — forgive ourselves for our foolishness. In the secret courtroom of our heart, we have prosecuted and convicted ourselves, and the penalty is a life sentence of self-hatred.

- Amy continued to party and use drugs during her pregnancy, and her child was born with a birth defect.
- Lucy underwent an abortion, which she later regretted.
- Ted argued with his son and ordered the teenager out of the house. Later that night, the boy was killed in a car wreck.
- John and his father had always shared a stormy relationship. John craved his father's approval, but felt he never measured up. The older man died suddenly and John

157

realized that his resentments had kept him from ever telling his father that he truly loved him. Now, it was too late. Is there any way to recover from such devastating guilt? Can we transform our pain? Can we heal?

A lot of us are ashamed of our feelings — and of ourselves — and this shame makes us secretive and closed. It is the rigidity of our closed-down stance that prevents healing from taking place. Healing is not easy. It requires a stark confrontation with reality, with our utter powerlessness to go back and correct the past, with our inability to make the world 100 percent safe and secure for ourselves and for those we love.

If we can acknowledge that powerlessness . . . if we can talk about it with others who understand . . . and if we can forgive ourselves for not being able to protect ourselves and the people we love from the unpredictable pain of living . . . if we can do these things, the effect can be truly liberating.

But why, you might ask, should you even consider forgiving yourself? Don't you deserve to be punished for your badness?

Indeed, a cogent argument could be made to support that idea, but consider this: The suffering you experience is only a fraction of the long-term pain caused by your guilt and remorse. When you experience depression, you think you are suffering alone, but you are wrong. The people who love you — your parents, lover, spouse, children, friends — suffer right along with you. When your pain doesn't stop, the joy is drained from their lives, too. Every person you come into contact with becomes infected in either a small or a large way by your unresolved pain.

When we refuse to embrace forgiveness, our relationships with other people are based on old hurts — not on love, not on caring, not on good judgment. Now ask yourself: Is punishing yourself for your past mistakes worth the pain it is causing today for you and your children or parents or mate?

What's done is done. You cannot undo it. If you constantly think about the past, you destroy your present and your future, too, because guilt is a constant barrier to love.

So, what can you do?

The first step in healing is to admit to ourselves that we are in deep emotional pain, that we hurt, and that we deeply regret the actions that have scarred us.

The second step is to accept our own powerlessness. Once we understand this, our guilt dissipates. We don't need to torture ourselves with statements like, "I should have known better." "I should have done better." "I should have been there." "I should have been able to do something."

If we could have done better, we would have. This is so hard for us to accept. We want to believe that we have within us the power to control ourselves and the world around us at all times. We want to believe if only we make the right decisions, we can always be safe. This is not true.

A friend named Karen was driving her son home from school one day when she was hit broadside by a car that ran a stop sign. She was not seriously hurt, but her son was killed.

This enormous tragedy devastated Karen. "If only I'd picked him up five minutes earlier," she cried. "If I'd been exactly on time, I would have been through that intersection. We would have been home and safe and he'd still be alive. It's my fault. I was so involved with myself that I was late getting him and now he's dead."

As the years passed, her grief did not abate. She kept blaming herself. "If only . . . if only . . . if only . . ." Those words haunted Karen every day and she grew more depressed, withdrawn, and self-destructive. Her guilt was killing her.

Blinded by her inner agony, Karen failed to see the pain her unrelenting self-hatred caused for the rest of her family. They not only had to bear their own grief; they also had to cope with Karen's guilt-induced self-destructiveness. Her surviving children became the innocent victims of Karen's bitterness, shame, and flaming anger.

Karen blamed herself for the death of her son. Yet, in reality, she could no more have predicted or prevented the accident that claimed his life than a leaf could predict the windstorm which rips it from its tree. Some things in life are random, unpredictable, and inevitable. We cannot control these tragedies, we cannot choose who is to suffer and who is to be spared, we do not have within us the ability to make everything come out all right for those we treasure.

Karen based her guilt on the wrong notion that she should have somehow been strong enough and powerful enough to foresee and control the tragic twistings and turnings of life. She kept telling herself that had she only been good enough, wise enough, or pleasing enough to God, then her family would have been spared.

This thinking is faulty. It is based on the infantile belief that we are solely responsible for all the good and bad things taking place around us. Cognitive therapists call this distorted thinking pattern *personalization.* We assume the blame for accidents, illnesses, and disasters when, in reality, we had no control over these events. We take on a burden of guilt because our ego tells us we should be capable of doing something, anything, to make unpredictable events come out right. Our refusal to accept our powerlessness causes our irrational guilt and blazing anger.

To heal, we must let go of the wrong notion that we can control everything that happens. To forgive ourselves, we must accept our human limitations. We cannot undo the past.

What can we do? We can learn our lessons, that's all. We don't have to repeat the same pattern over again.

No Storybook Endings

We know a man named Richard who made a complete mess of his life until he was almost 50 years old. He married young and had three children by the time he was 25. He was also an alcoholic. He made a good living as a mason and turned a large portion of his paychecks over to his wife, but other than that, he totally neglected his family. The only emotion he showed his children was anger. His sons grew up hating him.

Richard got sober when he was 47 years old, but by then it was too late to save his marriage. His wife divorced him. "I felt just terrible about what I'd put my family through," he said, recalling his former life. "Once I sobered up, I could see how I'd damaged my sons. I wanted to make it up to them, but they would have none of it. They rejected me totally."

Six years later, Richard married a woman who had two teenagers. At first, Richard treated his stepsons just like he'd treated his own boys — ordering them about, criticizing them, yelling at them when they didn't do their chores perfectly. As the conflict between Richard and the boys increased, so did Richard's feelings of futility and depression. He was angry all the time and he blamed his surliness on his stepsons.

After only a few months, his new wife threatened him with divorce. "Richard," she said, "I know that inside you is a good and kind and loving man. I know it, because I've seen it. That's the man I love. But I can't stand the hateful, mean person you turn into around my kids. That man is a stranger to me. I don't know what's wrong with you, but I do know I don't want to be married to you unless you are willing to change."

"I was real messed up," Richard confessed later. "You see, the only way I could bear the guilt of what I'd done to my own sons was to tell myself the problems were their fault, not mine. So, because of my guilt, I had this real high stake in not changing the way I raised kids. It was like treating my stepkids differently than I had treated my own sons would be an open admission that I had been wrong. I wasn't ready to face that, so I refused to change."

But the fear of losing his new family forced Richard to examine his life. For the first time, he admitted to himself that being rejected by his own sons had wounded him far more deeply than he had ever let on. Even more difficult was accepting the fact that they had rejected him with good cause. He had been a wretched father. A few years of sobriety could not make up for 30 years of abuse. Expecting a storybook ending after years of conflict was not realistic. But, on the other hand, *he didn't have to keep repeating his past mistakes in order to justify them.*

"I finally realized I didn't have to continue the pattern with my second family that had so badly hurt my first family. I could change."

And he did. He made peace with his new wife and his stepsons. They had a few sessions of family counseling together, and Richard continued in individual counseling to help him learn how to cope with his new feelings.

"I may never reconcile with my own sons," Richard admits. "All I can do is keep the channels of communication open to them and wait. At Christmas I sent a card with a letter inside. It was short and to the point. I told them I recognized that I had not been a very good father and that I was sorry. I told them I loved them and asked them to say a prayer for me. My youngest boy sent me a card back, so maybe we're making a little progress. And I'm getting along okay with my stepsons. It's hard sometimes, but I'm determined not to make the same mistakes twice."

Richard learned the hard way that old guilt can easily poison a new life. "If I could say one thing to people who have really messed up their lives it would be, please, don't repeat the same pattern all over again. You don't have to remain a prisoner to the past."

Appreciating this point gives us the opportunity to change our lives. If we look beyond our pain, recognize our wrongs, and work toward correcting our mistakes, we have the right to forgive ourselves and get on with living.

Others may never forgive us. And we have no right to demand their forgiveness. That's an unpleasant fact of life we may have to learn to accept.

But *we can heal ourselves if we will let go of the past.* By doing so, we can break down the barriers of self-hate that have kept us from accepting and giving the love that makes life worth living.

In the end, all that is left to us is forgiveness, for ourselves and for those who have hurt us. Only through forgiveness can we master life's most devastating circumstances, only by letting go of our guilt can we heal.

To forgive is to taste freedom for the first time. And in that freedom, we begin a healing transformation. For guilt is the cancer of life . . . and forgiveness its only cure.

Antidepressant Medication

In the classic tragedy *Macbeth*, Shakespeare touched on the perennial cry for something — anything — that will give the depressed person some relief. Lady Macbeth had gone mad and Macbeth asks a doctor for help:

Canst thou not minister to a mind diseased,
Pluck from the memory a rooted sorrow,
Raze out the written troubles of the brain,
And with some sweet oblivious antidote
Cleanse the stuffed bosom of that perilous stuff
That weighs upon the heart?

In Shakespeare's time there was no "sweet oblivious antidote" for depression. Today, however, drugs are now produced with greater technological skill than ever before. Developments in biochemical research have enabled scientists to manipulate molecules and to produce drugs that have a specific effect in a specific place in the nervous system. The precision engineering of antidepressants, however, leaves much to be desired. Antidepressants have a wide variety of side effects, and dosages must be carefully monitored.

In a very real sense, the use of antidepressant medication is a controlled experiment, with no certainty about the effectiveness and with many unknowns. But this is true of many drugs, and it is to be expected when we take into account the vast degree of biological differences among people. We are not standardized biological specimens cut out of DNA and protoplasm by a people-shaped cookie-cutter. Our biochemical equipment bears a family resemblance to the biochemical equipment of others, but the resemblance leaves a great deal of room for variety and uniqueness.

Despite the unknowns in drug therapy, in many instances the new antidepressant drugs have had a dramatic impact on depressions that have remained untouched by years of psychotherapy. Dr. Nathan S. Kline cites the case of a prominent radio personality who was manic-depressive. He was treated by a psychoanalyst for fifteen years, and all the time his moods vacillated from high to low, from elation to despair. "I think the analysis was invaluable," he later told Dr. Kline. "I gained a lot of insight into myself. I was probably the most insightful manic-depressive you ever met. But I was still a manic-depressive and had all my symptoms." Dr. Kline placed the man on medication and the symptoms were cleared up in about two months.

There's no question that antidepressant drugs have proved to be a valuable tool in combating depression. Even so, it is important to remember that there is no "magic bullet" for all depressions, no happy pill that will quickly and reliably banish the blues, pluck a rooted sorrow from memory, and erase the written troubles of the brain.

Drugs Do More Than One Thing

It is important to keep in mind one fact about drugs: Every form of medication always does more than one thing. Aspirin relieves headaches, but it also irritates the lining of the stomach. Antihistamines relieve symptoms of allergy and hay fever, but they also raise the blood pressure and cause drowsiness.

So it is with antidepressant medication. That's why it's critical to be conservative about using medication and to carefully monitor all symptoms and side effects arising from use of the drug itself or from drug interactions.

166

Now, let's take a quick look at the drugs found to be most effective in dealing with depression.

Tricyclic Antidepressants

Brand Names: Asendin, Elavil, Sinequan, Tofranil, Vivactil

Comments: Do not mix with any form of alcohol — beer, wine, or liquor. May counteract the effects of blood pressure medication. Tricyclics also interact with anticoagulants and thyroid medication. Discontinue at least two weeks before trying other forms of antidepressants. Always keep your physician informed about your drug use history and about the effects (both positive and negative) of the drug you are taking.

MAO (Mono-amine-oxidase) Inhibitors

Brand Names: Nardil, Marplan, Parnate

Comments: Certain foods must be avoided — especially aged cheeses and cured meats and fish. Other dietary restrictions: no bananas, avocadoes, raisins, chocolate, coffee or other caffeine-containing products. Dosage must be rigidly controlled and patients must be forewarned about possible hypertension crises — acute attacks of high blood pressure.

Lithium Chloride

Brand Name: Eskalith, Lithane, Lithium Carbonate, Lithobid

Comments: Generally prescribed for manic-depressive illness. Lithium affects the body's salt retention, so it should not be used with a salt-restricted diet. Drink lots of fluids. Regular tests must be taken throughout therapy to monitor the lithium level in the blood — even if there are no side effects detected.

Rules of Drug Dosage

Rule 1: *Don't take these drugs (or any other medications) without a prescription.* In other words, don't let a friend talk you into taking one of their pills when you feel down in the dumps. Taking a pill may sometimes act as a placebo and you may get a psychological lift from even a sugar pill. But antidepressants aren't sugar pills. They do not provide fast fast relief. They take time (perhaps up to two weeks or more) to do their biochemical work to relieve depression. A borrowed aspirin might ease the pain of a headache, but borrowed antidepressants can be real trouble.

Rule 2: *Report side effects to your physician immediately.* Ask your physician about potential side effects. If you experience unusual drowsiness, nausea, or another undesirable side effect get in touch with your doctor immediately. Similarly, if the drugs seem to have no effect after a couple of weeks, get back in touch with your physician. You may be taking the wrong drug, or you may be taking the wrong dosage.

Rule 3: *Don't mix and match your medicines for various ailments without your doctor's knowledge and permission.* Some drugs may work in combination with antidepressants to cause physical or psychological problems. Never take tranquilizers or amphetamines in combination with antidepressants. Every time your doctor writes you a prescription, remind him or her that you are taking antidepressants and ask what side effects or interactions you should watch out for when you add the new prescription on top of the old one. These simple questions are an important safeguard against possible unpleasant side effects.

Never use alcohol or other so-called "recreational drugs" — such as cocaine or marijuana — when you are being treated for depression. The results can be disastrous!

Rule 4. *Do not take drugs for depression when the depression results from normal sadness.* As we have said repeatedly, it is natural and normal to experience periods of sadness and grief in response to the "necessary losses" in life. It is tempting to escape sorrow and sadness by using some kind of mind- and emotion-numbing drug.

At a community drug abuse seminar Alice, a 67-year-old widow, disclosed that her doctor had tried to give her a prescription for tranquilizers when her husband died. "I didn't want the drugs," she said. "I felt bad about losing my husband, and I felt it was natural to feel bad. I loved him and I miss him, and wanted to feel bad about his death. I didn't want to be a drugged-up zombie with a foolish smile on my face pretending that I didn't feel deeply about losing the most important person in my life."

Rule 5. *Avoid use of antidepressants and other drugs during pregnancy.*

Rule 6. *Drugs alone may not "cure" depression.* Even though drugs can help regulate messed-up body chemistry, the misery mind-set may remain undiminished. The most effective treatment in many cases will consist of a combination of antidepressant drugs and the development of a new set of attitudes toward life.

Recent research shows that *cognitive therapy* is as effective as antidepressants in relieving depression. Keep in mind that there is no surefire cure-all for every form of depression. For depressions lasting longer than six weeks, a combination of cognitive therapy and antidepressant medication will likely be helpful.

In Chapter Four we stressed the importance of being honest with your physician. But it's also important to ask questions about the treatment your doctor prescribes. Dr. Hugh Drummond, a maverick psychiatrist, works in a mental health clinic in a low income industrial area. His advice in dealing with physicians:

> All I want you to do is feel a little less powerless and passive when the great god Asculapius walks into the room and tells you to drop your pants. You ought to learn that there is nothing sacred about medicine, and that if your doctor cannot tolerate some straightforward questions and even some challenges about his or her assumptions, then you should find a new doctor.

Before you go doctor shopping, make sure you are really following the advice of your current physician. One of the main problems in the treatment of depression is the tendency of the depressed person to abandon treatment — to give up because nothing seems to be happening or because progress is too slow.

All therapy takes time and it takes active participation. One of the biggest problems physicians encounter is the failure of patients to comply with recommended treatment. This is especially true of depressed patients, who often quit taking medication before it has a chance to work — or take the wrong dose of medication, or mix their medication with alcohol or other drugs.

If your physician prescribes medication, take it as prescribed — in the proper quantity for the recommended length of time. Note the changes, and keep your physician informed at all times about side effects.

Appendix B

Suicide: The Romance and the Reality

Many have commented on the tendency to romanticize suicidal depression. In the wake of Goethe's eighteenth century novel, *The Sorrows of Young Werther*, Europe was swept with a wave of suicides by passionately melancholy young men, thwarted in love and, in the words of Keats, "half in love with easeful death."

More recently, suicide has been glorified by writers like Sylvia Plath. Her novel, *The Bell Jar*, featured a heroine whose own instability made suicide seem a romantic and courageous solution to spiritual distress. The Japanese, wrote Plath, "understood things of the spirit."

They disemboweled themselves when anything went wrong. I tried to imagine how they would go about it. They must have an extremely sharp knife. No, probably two sharp knives. Then they would sit down, cross-legged, a knife in either hand. Then they would cross their hands and point a knife at each side of the stomach. They would have to be naked or the knife would get stuck in their clothes.

Then in one quick flash, before they had time to think twice, they would jab the knives in, and zip them round, one on the upper crescent and one on the lower crescent, making a full circle. Then their stomach skin would come loose, like a plate, and their insides would fall out, and they would die.

It must take a lot of courage to die like that.

In a much quoted poem ("Lady Lazarus"), Sylvia Plath continued her autobiographical flirtation with suicide:

Dying
Is an art, like everything else.
I do it exceptionally well.

True to her art, Plath finally committed suicide successfully, after several previous attempts.

The Grisly Secret of Suicide

There has been much speculation about reasons for suicide — many theories, many explanations. Suicide can be viewed as a cry for help, as a romantic gesture of self-renunciation, or as a spiteful act of supreme vengeance — in a sense, a willful triumph over real or imagined enemies, and a spit in the eye of God. But all too often the grisly reality of suicidal behavior remains a much guarded secret.

The reality is this: *Suicide is not a tidy solution*. The suicide inevitably leaves an ugly mess behind — in psychological and physical terms — for someone else to clean up. In the words of sociologist Lionel Tiger, the aftermath of suicide is a "legacy of pain."

Tiger remarks that suicide is "vicious, distorted, unbearably painful to family and friends, and a gross violation of the tentative truce with mortality which all humans must make." Tiger goes on to say, "Suicides . . . make a major statement about the value of life and thus call into question the very source of optimistic gregariousness which sustains us all."

Writing on suicide in the *CoEvolution Quarterly*, Art Kleiner comments:

I suspect suicidal people are automatically rescued not for their own sakes, but for the rest of us. A suicide death, unless it is rationally prepared for, devastates. The message of a suicide attempt is often: Death is better than the pain you've caused me.

Tiger, the author of *Optimism: The Biology of Hope*, had a close friend and colleague who killed himself. Tiger was the last person to see the man alive, and recalls, "I cannot begin to describe the profoundly demoralizing effect his suicide had on those of us around him." The impact was all the more demoralizing because the suicide victim was "an extraordinarily talented, charming, seductive and psychologically dramatic professor."

Years later the chairman of Tiger's department disclosed he had recommended that Tiger be given a year's leave of absence because the chairman believed Tiger was gravely depressed and needed to escape the blight of what had happened. "Was his diagnosis correct?" asks Tiger. "I think so, although I wasn't aware of the degree of my despondency then."

Such deep and soul-searching despondency is common in the people the suicide leaves behind. "When suicides occur," Tiger reflects, "we all claim responsibility or feel we share in the failure of the social fabric to support the person in need." Was there something we could have done or said to prevent the person from taking that last final step into oblivion? Did we ignore the obvious signs, did we bother to find out how depressed the person was? Did we fail to take the depression seriously and think it was "just a phase"? These questions and more run through the minds of the friends and loved ones left behind.

But there's another aspect of suicide that undermines the foundations of our own lives. The suicide attempt devastates and fascinates us because it reminds us how fragile our hold on life really is. We struggle along with our problems, and the suicide just seems to put it all aside, saying, "It isn't worth the struggle. Good-bye, cruel world." It's a shocking repudiation of the high value most of us place on life. The suicide tosses life aside like so much trash. As Tiger puts it, "Suicide is a violent challenge to our general complacency about the extraordinary value of life. To be sure, suicide is not only violent against the community but also against the survivors."

This might be called the psychological legacy of pain. But there's another legacy of pain that most suicides never take into consideration — the legacy of a broken, battered, blood- and excrement-soaked body drowning in vomit, clinging to life in spite of all the good intentions about a sanitized and uncomplicated self-deliverance.

Just as alcohol and other drug abuse have been glamorized in the past by showing the use of drugs *without real-life consequences,* so suicide has frequently been depicted as a swift, painless, and uncomplicated solution to life's problems. An extreme solution, to be sure, but an awesome and perhaps courageous step into the void.

What more people need to know is that suicide is most often the pathetic act of a confused and desperate person. If we look at the real-life consequences of suicide and suicide attempts, we find that the seemingly antiseptic solution turns out to be messy and unpredictable.

In the words of an advocate of rational self-deliverance, more people need to know "how not to commit suicide."

Little Known Hazards of Suicide

The theme song from the movie *M*A*S*H* is titled "Suicide," and the lyrics go: "Suicide is painless, It brings on many changes. . . ."

However, suicide does not always bring on swift, painless, sweet oblivion. The attempt sometimes gets all botched up and the would-be suicide suffers a good deal of pain and disfigurement.

Most suicides and suicide attempts take the form of drug overdoses. Art Kleiner describes what happens:

The danger in all drug overdoses is that the brain may not get enough oxygen. The airway to the lungs may get blocked off by the patient's vomit, or by the tongue falling back into the throat, or by drug-induced slow-down in the part of the deep brain that controls the rate and depth of breathing.

Permanent brain damage occurs when the brain is deprived of oxygen for three to five minutes. Higher brain functions are the first to go — memory is destroyed, verbal skills are impaired — and the longer the oxygen starvation goes on, the more severe the retardation.

Aspirin is one of the most common drugs used in botched suicide attempts, probably because of its wide availability and our ignorance about the terminal effectiveness of an overdose. One pharmacologist calls aspirin "one of the messiest, most complicated overdoses you ever hope to see." Aspirin can burn the gastrointestinal tract and can damage the kidneys, lungs, and liver. Aspirin in sufficient quantity can produce a fever and seizures. People who survive aspirin overdoses can suffer permanent liver damage and sometimes suffer deafness or tinnitus (ringing in the ears).

Tylenol (or acetaminophen) poisoning also destroys the liver. This can result in an especially painful death because patients often sleep off the initial sickness, recover enough to realize they didn't really want to die, then slowly slip off into a coma after five days because the liver has been destroyed.

Sedatives and alcohol are a common and dangerous combination in suicide attempts. When taken together, alcohol and Valium, Seconal, or other sedatives and mild tranquilizers produce nausea and vomiting. Instead of drifting off into death, the suicidal person sucks vomit into the lungs. If the person doesn't drown in vomit, they can become infected and develop pneumonia and irreversible lung damage.

The most painful form of a suicide attempt is swallowing lye, Drano, oven cleaner, or some other form of household caustic agent. Very few people die from swallowing lye or other caustics. "If they do die," says one physician, "it's days, weeks, or even months later, of infection." Caustics like lye burn the mouth, tongue, and may burn holes through the esophagus and into the chest cavity. The resulting scar tissue can obstruct the gastrointestinal tract, and patients may have to undergo years of painful corrective surgery.

"Violent death is so often portrayed as sudden and painless," Kleiner reports, "but the human body is harder to kill than it seems." Slitting the wrists, for example, rarely results in death. More often, tendons and nerves are damaged, and the would-be suicide ends up with a weak or deformed hand.

Those who cut their throats rarely die. They cut the nerve that controls their voice box and larynx and end up voiceless. Gunshot wounds can kill outright, but, remarkably enough, people frequently miss the brain and blow out an eye or part of a jaw. People can live for hours with a hole in the head the size of a half dollar. Says one physician, "One man I treated is completely paralyzed on his left side, and can't speak, walk, or feed himself. It's as if he had a major stroke. He hit the area of the brain which controls motor function."

While brain death comes fairly rapidly with oxygen deprivation, the brain can survive bizarre assaults. One man tried to kill himself by hammering eleven nails into the top of his head. Finding himself still alive, he walked to the hospital and presented himself to the emergency ward.

Hanging seems to offer a fairly rapid demise, but those who try to hang themselves may dangle and slowly choke. They don't always die but, like other failed suicides, end up with irreversible brain damage.

Jumping from a high place can cause a nonfatal, but painful and permanent injury. In 1986, a world-class runner dropped out of the middle of a race and jumped off a bridge. She did not kill herself, but her jump caused irreversible injuries — she is now quadriplegic. According to those who have studied suicide attempts, people can fall over a hundred feet — and sometimes more — without killing themselves. Jumpers who survive suffer multiple fractures — crushed and shattered bones — and ruptured internal organs. Because of the fragility of the spine and brain, jumpers may be left totally paralyzed.

Botched suicides happen so frequently and have such unexpected and unseemly consequences that Dr. George B. Mair, a British advocate of rational self-deliverance, wrote a book on suicidal etiquette called *How To Die With Dignity*. Dr. Mair cautions:

- It is exceptionally unwise to attempt to jump in front of trains, motor buses, or other vehicles. Results are unpredictable.
- Jumping into the sea from the ferry or other deep sea vessel is highly inconvenient for the ship's crew and passengers.
- Attempts to crash a car even moving at a very high speed is extremely uncertain and should be avoided.
- Jumping onto the live rail of an electric rail system is not in any way dignified and is a great offense to witnesses.

In her poem "Resume," Dorothy Parker made some wry observations about various drawbacks of suicide techniques:

Razors pain you;
Rivers are damp;
Acids stain you;
And drugs cause cramp.
Guns aren't lawful;
Nooses give;
Gas smells awful;
You might as well live.

Rational Suicide?

Many students of depression and suicidal behavior have commented on the "rational suicide." Given the fact that most suicides leave a legacy of pain, there is another aspect to be considered: Some suicides appear to be well thought-out solutions to intolerable problems. From an outsider's point of view, the solution of suicide may not necessarily seem to be the best solution, but it is perhaps better, in the suicide's eye, than the perceived alternatives. Many students of depression and suicidal behavior have remarked on the "rational suicide."

Aaron Beck, a psychologist who has written extensively on depression, observes that depression stems from the cognitive stance the depressed person takes toward the world. The depressed person's expectations are permeated with negativity, and he or she sees only continued unhappiness and hopelessness on into the future. Rather than face such a future, the suicide opts to turn away from a painfully futile existence.

"He cannot visualize any way of improving things," says Beck. "He does not believe it is possible to get better. Suicide under these conditions seems to the patient to be a rational solution."

The Thanatos Society and similar groups give individuals support for the choice of suicide under intolerable conditions such as terminal illness.

Of course, what one person considers to be intolerable, another person might readily tolerate. In E. A. Robinson's well-known poem, Richard Cory was "a gentleman from sole to crown, / Clean favored and imperially slim." He was rich and well-schooled in every grace. He "fluttered pulses when he said, / Good morning, and he glittered when he walked."

In fine, we thought that he was everything
To make us wish we were in his place.

But Robinson's poem comes to an ironic conclusion:

So on we worked, and waited for the light,
And went without the meat, and cursed the bread,
And Richard Cory, one calm summer night
Went home and put a bullet in his head.

When a Nebraska farmer committed suicide, a friend reflected, "That last day seemed like all the others. I never knew how bad it was for him. Pete never let on. He was cheerful, he ate turkey sandwiches with me, and then he killed himself."

Mary, Pete's wife, had no idea he had been plotting his

suicide for six months or more. "I lived with a man who was planning to kill himself and I didn't notice any signals. I look back now, and I still don't see any signs. I worried about heart attacks and car wrecks. I didn't think about interest rates, foreclosures or bankruptcy. But that's what killed Pete."

Pete was not immobilized by depression. Quite the opposite. He left a set of instructions about how to organize the funeral (along with a detailed script for his own funeral, including friends to notify and pallbearers). He also left elaborate suggestions about how to deal with bankers, bill collectors and other creditors, as well as insurance agents. He entered his wife's name in the new telephone book as president of their corporate ranch. He prepaid her dues at the country club for the next two years — again without her knowledge. He filled in chores to be done on the pages of the next year's calendar. And he bought Christmas gifts for his wife and kids, to be delivered by friends.

No doubt Pete thought his elaborate preparations would make his death less traumatic. But his death shocked and devastated those closest to him. Would prepaid dues at the country club compensate for the loss of a husband? Would Christmas presents delivered by a third party really be any consolation for the loss of a father? What made him think it would be easier for his wife to deal with creditors than it was for him?

For all of his apparent concern for the future of his family, Pete was capable of enormous deception and irrational self-justification — a sure sign of the distorted logic of the suicide. His "solution" solved nothing; it only created unspeakable pain for his survivors.

Another example of the twisted covert thinking of the suicide can be seen in a beleaguered Wyoming farmer who also killed himself without any warning. His wife said his decision must have been a long time in the making. "In all our years together I never had to pick up a sock. He was very orderly and methodical. That day, for the first time in weeks, he didn't seem worried. He was in control. As he left the house, he turned around in the yard and came back three times to kiss me."

His wife asked if he was okay, and he said, "I love you very much." That was the last time she saw him alive. She has a long time to reflect on the kind of love that leaves behind immeasurable grief and confusion.

Psychiatrist William Glasser reports on one seventeen-year-old boy who committed suicide:

> In a typical case, the parents of a seventeen-year-old boy thought in retrospect, he spent more time by himself than seemed normal. In school, where his work was satisfactory, what was noticeable was that he was not noticed; he tended to blend into the background. He did have a few close friends, and he did not complain that anything major was wrong. Obviously, he must have been suffering from a huge and growing perceptual error; the life he wanted was not at all working out. Even though he appeared outwardly calm, we believe that disturbing ideas that had never been there before were racing through his mind. More and more the idea that life was overwhelmingly painful crowded out other thoughts. To relieve the pain, he threw a rope over the garage rafter, fixed it around his neck, and stepped off the chair.

But the boy did not understand that *suicide is forever, not just for the victim, but for those around the victim — the friends, children, and parents.* For they are the ones left with the suicide's legacy of pain.

Evaluating Suicidal Risk

How can one tell whether a person is suicidal or not? There is no way to predict with absolute certainty that an individual is a suicide risk. But there are a number of indicators that show up fairly often in high risk individuals. Consider these questions when trying to assess the risk for suicide:

1. Have there been previous attempts?
2. Has the person been preoccupied with thoughts of death — rather than just casual thoughts of suicide?
3. Have there been any recent deaths or losses?
4. Has the individual spoken of a plan to commit suicide, or talked about a specific method of suicide?
5. Has the person recently and unexpectedly finalized business, or written or revised a will?
6. Does the person live alone — with few friends, contacts?
7. Is there a family history of suicide?
8. Does the person have a history of alcohol problems or other forms of chemical dependency?
9. Has the person ever had psychiatric treatment or hospitalization for pronounced mood changes?
10. Has the person expressed feelings of unreality?
11. Does the person suffer from severe illness with unremitting pain accompanied by strong feelings of depression?
12. Were previous attempts serious with little likelihood of rescue or survival?

A "yes" answer to two or more of the above questions indicates a high risk of suicide.

Suicide Prevention

How about suicide prevention? Most suicide prevention workers feel that suicidal people haven't examined all the alternatives to suicide. Those who work on telephone crisis hot lines try to get the caller to consider alternatives.

One worker speaks about the "tunnel vision" of suicidal callers. "Usually it hasn't dawned on them who it will affect or what the long-range effects of their act will be. Once they realize it, they often don't want the suicide to happen. They don't want to die; they want the pain to stop."

When dealing with the depressed person, most of us tend to tippy-toe around the topic of suicide. There's a hidden agenda that goes, "Let's don't talk about it." Or: "I won't bring it up if you won't." We are often afraid to ask depressed people if they are considering suicide, because we think that somehow it might give them ideas, it might trigger a suicidal gesture. We are trapped by the myths about suicide.

Myths About Suicide

Myth: People who talk about suicide do not commit suicide.

Fact: Talkers are often doers. Threats should be taken seriously.

Myth: Suicide happens without warning.

Fact: Suicides talk about hopelessness and the suicidal solution. They make threats — some veiled, some overt. They may talk about death fantasies or express the feeling, "They'll be sorry when I die." In general, the more specific the threat (as to method of suicide, time, place, etc.) the greater the probability of a real, serious attempt.

Myth: Suicidal people are fully intent on dying.

Fact: The man who jumped into the cactus patch said, "It seemed like a good idea at the time." So it is with suicides. Suicide may seem like a good idea at the time, but many suicidal people appreciate the opportunity to reconsider. A man who survived a suicidal jump from the Golden Gate Bridge says he realized he was making a horrible mistake when his hands slipped from the railing and he plunged 249 feet into the Bay. A year later, he told a reporter he was "thrilled to be alive," and he urged others thinking about suicide to give life another chance.

Myth: Once a person is suicidal, he or she is suicidal forever.

Fact: People who feel suicidal or who actually attempt suicide may find ways to strengthen their resolve to live and may put all thoughts of suicide entirely behind them, going on to live happy and productive lives.

Myth: Improvement following a suicidal crisis means the suicidal risk is over.

Fact: The mood change from suicidal depression to apparent tranquility may in fact reflect that a person has reached a decision to commit suicide. Having reached a decision, the burden of living is lifted, leaving room for a serenity that may mislead others into thinking the crisis has passed.

Myth: Suicide strikes more often among the rich, or almost exclusively among the poor.

Fact: The will to live appears to be distributed equally among all economic levels of the population.

Most experts who have studied suicide agree that it's essential to dispel the myths and lift the taboos around talking about suicide. People who are suicidally depressed should be confronted about their suicidal ideas and they should be encouraged to look at alternatives. "Don't argue with them about why life is worth living because you can't win that one," says Kleiner. Tell them something more concrete, more personal. "Tell them how you and other people will feel when they're gone. If there are mental health services you trust in your neighborhood, you may want to suggest them."

When free-lance journalist Karen Lindsey became suicidal, friends rallied to bolster her flagging motivation to continue living.

No one tried to deny or judge my suicidal feelings, but Byrna was especially good at talking about suicide as a practical decision. How much physical pain could I endure? How was I going to carry it out? Was I sure I could do it without botching it and ending up alive and paralyzed or brain damaged? Could I do it in such a way that my body wasn't discovered by someone who loved me and would be traumatized for life?

Karen Lindsey appreciated this straightforward, reality-based focus on suicide. Her friend Byrna spoke about the unspeakable, bringing up all the unpleasant details, grisly secrets, and uncontemplated hazards of suicide. It may sound heartless, but Karen found the discussion to be helpful.

It demystified suicide, taking it out of the realm of guilt and sentiment and making it what it was: a totally serious and irrevocable decision which I had the right to make, but was responsible — both to myself and my friends — for making clearheadedly.

What about suicide prevention services? Do they help? The data is sketchy. Studies show that these services in the United States have failed to produce the hoped for reduction in suicide rates in the locales where they have been developed. The harsh fact remains: "People who are sure about killing themselves rarely call the suicide hot line." These are what some researchers have called "the true suicide constituency."

In the book *Suicide: Theory and Clinical Aspects*, L. D. Hankoff and Bernice Einsidler report:

Mass information approaches which emphasize telephone hot lines may be profitable for alcoholism and acute emotional upsets, but some other means is needed for dealing with chronically and more malignantly suicidal individuals who account for the greater proportion of suicide fatalities and are probably the least responsive to hot line services.

In the end, we must candidly admit that suicide prevention is in its infancy. We can list endless reasonable arguments against suicide, but as writer Cesare Pavese, a member of the "true suicide constituency" (he committed suicide) once observed: "No one ever lacks a good reason for suicide."

But if given the opportunity, depressed people who think they have found a way to relieve their misery through suicide, might find that there are better means of relieving the misery . . . *by changing their lives instead of abandoning them.*

Appendix C

Suggested Readings

Feeling Good: The New Mood Therapy, by David D. Burns, M.D., Signet (New American Library), 1981.

One of the best discussions of the cognitive approach to overcoming mood disorders. Dr. Burns spells out ten types of twisted thinking, gives guidance on boosting self-esteem, and makes concrete suggestions on constructive ways of dealing with "approval addiction," guilt, and hostility that go hand in hand with depression.

In a chapter titled "Do-Nothingism: How to Beat It," Burns introduces a valuable concept: The Lethargy Cycle. Says Burns:

> Your self-defeating negative thoughts make you feel miserable. Your painful emotions in turn convince you that your distorted, pessimistic thoughts are actually valid. Similarly, self-defeating thoughts and actions reinforce each other in a circular manner.

The result is a state of near-paralysis, pessimism, and lethargy. "The unpleasant consequences of do-nothingism make your problems even worse."

Unlike many cognitive therapists, Burns recognizes the importance of integrating biochemical and cognitive approaches to overcoming depression and includes a valuable section on "A consumer's guide to antidepressant drug therapy."

The Pill Book of Anxiety and Depression, Bantam Books, 1985.

This book gives a short overview of current approaches to the treatment of anxiety and depression. It provides sections of general information about the most commonly prescribed anxiety and depression drugs in the United States, generic and brand names, with complete descriptions of the drugs and their effects.

In addition, *The Pill Book on Anxiety and Depression* includes appendices that list the varieties of physical illnesses and drugs that can cause symptoms of anxiety or symptoms of depression.

The Pill Book contains valuable basic information that underscores the multidimensional nature of depression.

Depression and Its Treatment, by John H. Greist, M.D. and James W. Jefferson, M.D., Warner Books, 1985

A short, down-to-earth discussion of depression, answering many of the most-asked questions about depression and treatment for depression, written without jargon — all of which makes this volume a good place to start learning more about depression, its causes and treatment.

Treatments of depression range from talk therapy to drug therapy and, in more severe cases, ECT (electroconvulsive shock). The authors point out that the use of exercise — most often a combination of walking and running — is becoming more common in the treatment of depression. But they caution that exercise has not been shown to be of benefit in "severe" depression.

The People's Pharmacy by Joe Graedon, St. Martin's Press, 1985.

Joe Graedon is a pharmacist who has been in the business of demystifying pills and giving consumers accurate, up-to-date information about the prescribed medications and over-the-counter nostrums commonly used and abused.

The People's Pharmacy includes a special section on antidepressant medications with an especially valuable section on
drug interactions titled "When 1 + 1 May Equal 3."

Graedon's book has a strong section on side effects of medications, including an eye-opening discussion of the side
effects most doctors won't mention — "Sexual Side Effects:
Doctors' Lips Are Sealed."

Graedon's message could be carried in a slogan found in
different forms throughout his book: "Drug Safety: Protect
the Bod — It's the Only One You've Got." It's a slogan that
can't be repeated too many times in our age of chemical fixes
for every ill.

Optimism: The Biology of Hope, by Lionel Tiger, Simon &
Schuster, 1979.

Lionel Tiger's study of optimisms, small and large, gives
the other side of the biochemistry of depression — and
shows how and why in humans "Hope Springs Internal."
Tiger provides some intriguing answers to the questions,
"How do nice ideas make people feel better, evidently even
in their bodies, and how do bad ideas, and bad threats of
things to come, cause them to feel bad, apparently even in
their bodies?"

Tiger places depression in an evolutionary perspective and
gives some thought-provoking observations about suicide.
Unfortunately, *Optimism: The Biology of Hope* is not a lucid
book and may be slow going for the average reader. It might
be seen as a sociology professor's version of *The Power of
Positive Thinking,* by Norman Vincent Peale. Nevertheless,
Tiger's writings are worth pursuing.

The Right To Feel Bad, by Lesley Hazleton, The Dial Press,
1984.

The subtitle of this book is "Coming to Terms with Normal
Depression." Unlike most writers on depression, Hazleton
raises many pointed questions about our eagerness to medi-
cate unhappiness, and to make a disease out of problems

of living.

For all of us, depression is basically a matter of personal politics. It belongs less to the realm of statistics and psychiatry than to that of our personal systems of belief — how we are to lead our lives, by what values, and on what level. It also relates to our personal morality.

One study found a "shockingly" high incidence of chronic depression among working class women in London. Hazleton points out that this is a perfect example of the social and cultural roots of normal depression.

It seems clear that in a society where many of the women have small children, are unemployed, have no stable partner, and live in substandard housing, depression will be endemic. They do not live in such situations because they are depressed; rather, they are depressed because of their situation. They would be very odd people if they were not.

On the real role of psychotherapy:

Few therapists today — whether psychiatrists, psychologists, analysts, or social workers — seem to have either the humor or the realism to appreciate Freud's remark that he cured the miseries of the neurotic only to open him up to the normal miseries of life.

You cannot cure life, Hazleton reminds those who search for the ultimate cure. It's impossible to live in the real world and feel good all the time.

Anatomy of Melancholy, by Robert Burton, 1621.

There are many editions of this classic compendium of the causes and cures of melancholy — as it was understood in the seventeenth century. It is an unusual book of great scholarship and contains a wealth of information on melancholy through the ages, as well as curious and sometimes helpful suggestions for coping with depression. Burton, who was himself afflicted with bouts of melancholia, wrote the book as an antidote to his own illness. One of his classic bits of advice: "Better do to no end, than nothing." It's a great temptation to become paralyzed with melancholy, says Burton. Do something, don't just mope like a turnip — melancholy wisdom, as pertinent and useful now as it was in the seventeenth century.

"How Not To Commit Suicide," by Art Kleiner *CoEvolution Quarterly*, no. 30, Summer 1981, pp. 88-109.

Kleiner's article does a commendable job in raising important, but often overlooked issues about suicide. Too frequently we treat suicide gingerly as if covertly following the old taboo: Don't speak ill of the dead. Kleiner breaks through this taboo by examining the real facts of suicide, rather than sanitized postmortems.

Especially recommended:

Any of the writings of Norman Vincent Peale, such as *The Power of Positive Thinking.* Peale has been scorned by many professionals (including the present authors) for years because of his somewhat simple-minded optimism. Nevertheless, Peale gives excellent advice on positive thinking and "tough-minded optimism." And his advice is grounded in reality to a greater extent than most of his critics believe.

Peale has a gift for lucid writing and for giving instructive, concrete examples that a broad spectrum of people can relate to. These qualities make him a classic writer in the self-help field, where writers often obfuscate with tedious technicality and obscure jargon.

While Peale has been a promoter of positive thinking for decades, he confesses in his autobiography that early in his career he suffered from bouts of inadequacy and discouragement. He thought he had a message for others, and put his ideas into a book. But publisher after publisher turned down the manuscript.

Finally, he became so dejected by the rejection of the book by publishers that he threw the manuscript in the trash. His wife rescued the book and, without Peale's knowledge, took it to a publisher. The book Peale's wife retrieved from the garbage can turned out to be the best-selling *The Power of Positive Thinking*.

Other Suggested Readings

A Season in Hell, Percy Knauth, Harper and Row, 1975.

Suicide Theory and Clinical Aspects, L. D. Hankoff and Bernice Einsidler, PSG Publishing Company, Littleton, Mass., 1979.

From Sad to Glad, Nathan S. Kline, M.D., Ballantine Books, 1975.

The Savage God, A. Alvarez, Random House, 1970.